PLAYMAKERS REPERTORY COMPANY

A HISTORY

PLAYMAKERS REPERTORY COMPANY

A History

EDITED BY BOBBI OWEN

ADAM VERSÉNYI, ADVISORY EDITOR

UNIVERSITY OF NORTH CAROLINA AT CHAPEL HILL
DEPARTMENT OF DRAMATIC ART

PlayMakers Repertory Company: A History

Edited by Bobbi Owen; Adam Versényi, Advisory Editor

Set in Garamond Premier Pro by Copperline Book Services, Inc.

Manufactured in the United States of America

Library of Congress Cataloging-in-Publication Data

Names: Owen, Bobbi, editor. | Versényi, Adam, editor.
Title: PlayMakers Repertory Company : a history / edited by Bobbi Owen ;
    Adam Versényi, advisory editor.
Description: [Chapel Hill] : University of North Carolina Department of
    Dramatic Art, [2021] | Includes index. | Foreword: The Bow Tie / by
    Brian Hargrove – Preface / by Bobbi Owen – Introduction / by Adam
    Versényi – In the Beginning: Tom Haas / by Bobbi Owen – New Voices
    and Big Ideas: David Rotenberg and Gregory Boyd / by Cecelia Moore –
    New Horizons: Milly S. Barranger and David Hammond ; Beyond Borders:
    Joseph Haj / by Gregory Kable – Resolutely Engaging the Future:
    Vivienne Benesch / by Cecelia Moore – Afterword / by Vivienne Benesch
    – Appendix I: PlayMakers Repertory Company Productions, 1975-1976 to
    Present – Appendix II: Department of Dramatic Art Faculty, 1975-1976 to
    Present – Appendix III: MFA Degree Recipients, 1975 to Present –
    Appendix IV: PlayMakers Repertory Company Administrative Leadership,
    1975 to Present.
Identifiers: LCCN 2020055720 | ISBN 9781469665467 (paperback)
Subjects: LCSH: PlayMakers Repertory Company–History. | University of
    North Carolina at Chapel Hill. Department of Dramatic Art–History. |
    Theatrical companies–North Carolina–Chapel Hill–History. |
    Theater–Study and teaching (Higher)–North Carolina–Chapel
    Hill–History.
Classification: LCC PN2277.C295 P55 2021 | DDC 792.09756/565–dc23
LC record available at https://lccn.loc.gov/2020055720

ISBN 978-1-4696-6546-7 (paperback: alk. paper)

ISBN 978-1-4696-6547-4 (ebook)

COVER ILLUSTRATION: *Julius Caesar,* 2019–2020. Tia James as Mark Antony.
Costume Design by Grier Coleman, Set Design by Jan Chambers, Lighting Design
by Kate McGee. Photograph by HuthPhoto, Courtesy of PRC.

FRONTIS: *Metamorphoses*, 2013–2014. Maren Searle as First Woman. Costume and
Set Design by Jan Chambers and McKay Coble, Lighting Design by Marcus Dillard.
Photograph by Michal Daniel. Courtesy of PRC.

Published by the University of North Carolina Department of Dramatic Art

Distributed by the University of North Carolina Press

www.uncpress.org

CONTENTS

ILLUSTRATIONS

Once in a Lifetime, 1976–1977. Quartet and company members: Front row (*left to right*): Chip Arnold, Marnie Carmichael, Sandra Geiss-Karas, David Shepherd as the quartet. Back row (*left to right*): Brian Hargrove, Jule Selbo, Deborah Maxwell, Joan Finchley, John Chappell, Lisa Whalin, and Dave Rogers as Sailors, Marty Shapiro as Cameraman #1, Susan Bradford as Script Girl. Costume Design by Bobbi Owen, Set Design by Rick Pike, Lighting Design by David M. Glenn. Photograph by Howard Shepherd. Courtesy of PRC.

FOREWORD | THE BOW TIE

By Brian Hargrove

Not long ago, I was getting dressed to go to the Broadway opening of *It Shoulda Been You*—a new musical with book and lyrics by me (Brian Hargrove) and directed by my husband (David Hyde Pierce). We'd decided to wear tuxedos because at most Broadway openings, if the writer and director are not booed out of the theatre, they're invited on stage to bow with the cast, and we wanted to look good either way.

As I tied and retied my bow tie for the hundredth time, I thought back to 1974, where in the dimly-lit costume shop on the ground floor of the Graham Memorial Building on the UNC-Chapel Hill campus, I was first taught how to tie a bow tie. At the time, I didn't know how important that lesson would be—back then, I didn't know what I didn't know I didn't know.

When I arrived at Carolina in 1974, my plan was to earn an undergrad degree and get as much acting experience as possible. But the next year, Tom Haas and Arthur Housman converted the Carolina PlayMakers, an amateur theatre company, into PlayMakers Repertory Company, a professional Equity company, changing the whole focus of the Department of Dramatic Art at Chapel Hill.

As attention shifted to the new MFA program, many of us undergraduates were afraid we would get short shrift. (And by "we" I mean "me.") Adding insult to injury, we were now required to crew two shows with the newly formed PlayMakers Repertory Company. I "volunteered" to help out in the costume department because all I had to do was help some of the graduate students get dressed in formal wear for Ibsen's *The Wild Duck*. Easy, right? Except none of us knew how to tie a bow tie.

Enter Dave Rogers. Dave knew all about the clothes of the period because he was studying to be a costumer. (That's a real profession? Who knew? Apparently, everyone but me.) Soon after Dave initiated us in the art of "Tie Chi," I was helping people tie them upside down and sideways, and I began to realize that learning how and why other theatre artists did what they did might be good idea. And that was just the first lesson.

I was now given the chance to watch, work with, and get to know professionals from all over the country and the world. Bobbi Owen, a recent graduate of the University of Wisconsin, was brought in to overhaul the costume department. Over the years, she oversaw its growth into one of the most well-run and respected costume shops in the country—thanks to Judy Adamson, one of the greatest costume makers on the planet, and the help of lots of talented graduate students. Cecily Berry, the vocal coach for the Royal Shakespeare Company, was also brought in to give the voice and speech department a kick in the diphthongs.

My fear that we would be ignored proved unfounded. I was given opportunities that I never would have gotten anywhere else at any other time. When I was a lowly sophomore, I got the chance to work professionally with Tom Haas and the incredible actors that made up the original company of PlayMakers Rep: Dallas Greer, Maggie Tucker, Sandra Karas and Mina Penland to name a few. Being on stage with them was like getting a master class in acting every night.

Tom cast me in *Johnny Johnson*, a musical by Paul Green and Kurt Weill about World War I, as a young German soldier who Johnny (Dal Greer) meets on the battlefield. Dal, one of those rare actors who has the ability to *actually* listen, was a fantastic Johnny Johnson because he was an everyman—the kind of guy we all either wish we knew or wish we were. When he talked about the horrors of war, people paid attention.

I will never forget the way Tom staged the end of the show. We were performing at the original Playmakers Theatre, and the set was the backstage of the theatre itself, which had been painted gray to look like an old black and white photo from the period. On the back wall, slightly off-center, there was a small door that opened directly onto Cameron Avenue, the campus road that runs between the theatre and the Old Well. As each of the characters finished their last line (or in my case died), they would exit through that back door. Dal was the last actor on stage—he would wave goodbye, walk out the door, and leave it open. The lights would come up on the audience, the Stage Manager would wheel the ghost light to center stage, then walk out and shut the back door. That was it. Play over. No bows. Nothing.

The audience didn't know what to do. It was as still as death inside the theatre. That moment brought out our own feelings of isolation and uncertainty, capturing in essence the loneliness and emptiness of war. Tom was a genius. I only wish he were still around so I could tell him.

Experiences like that change you. They become part of, not only who you are, but who you will be. From tying a bow tie to crafting a show, the lessons of PlayMakers have stayed with me and nurtured me from Carolina to Juilliard, from acting to writing, from Hollywood to a Broadway opening.

When I was at Chapel Hill, I didn't know I was attending at the birth of a repertory company that would become a destination for some of this country's finest actors, playwrights, designers, and directors. Over the years, each artistic director has put their own indelible stamp on PlayMakers, keeping it current, important, and necessary.

For me and all the naïve, know-nothing kids who started out in Chapel Hill hoping to be something more than we could dream, we now have a place we can dream of returning to. As this book shows, though it's changed a lot since we left, PlayMakers is and will always be home.

A graduate of UNC-Chapel Hill and the Juilliard School, BRIAN HARGROVE began acting professionally in NYC, including appearances in *How It All Began* at the Public Theatre, *Henry IV* for Shakespeare in the Park, *Vieux Carré* at the WPA Theater, and *The Three Sisters* at the Manhattan Theatre Club. Regionally, he worked at Boston's Huntington Theatre, Indiana Repertory Theatre, A.C.T. Seattle, and the Guthrie Theater's 1985–1986 season, meanwhile shooting lots of TV commercials and serving as a president of Merely Players, a company showcasing recent UNC-Chapel Hill playwright/actor/director graduates. He moved to Hollywood, becoming a television writer/producer on *Dave's World, Caroline in the City, Holding the Baby, Maggie* and *Wanda at Large,* and co-creating/executive producing the hit FOX-TV show *Titus.* He wrote the book and subsequent NBC television movie *My Life as a Dog* (about Moose, the dog on *Frasier*) and co-wrote a new narration for Saint-Saëns' "Carnival of the Animals," which was performed at the Hollywood Bowl. With composer Barbara Anselmi, Brian wrote the book and lyrics to the original musical *It Shoulda Been You*, produced by Daryl Roth and directed by David Hyde Pierce, which opened April 14, 2015 at Broadway's Brooks Atkinson Theatre.

Once in a Lifetime, 1976–1977. Full company (fifty-six cast members—and one dog—remains the largest in PRC history to date and it was staged in the original Playmakers Theatre). Costume Design by Bobbi Owen, Set Design by Rick Pike, Lighting Design by David M. Glenn. Tom Haas is in the front row, fifth from the right. Photograph by Howard Shepherd. Courtesy of PRC.

PREFACE

By Bobbi Owen

When I joined the faculty in the Department of Dramatic Art at UNC-Chapel Hill in the fall of 1974, my dream was to be the resident costume designer in a professional regional theatre (once I had paid off my college bills). Lucky for me, PlayMakers Repertory Company (PRC) was formed here a year after I arrived, and thus—I got to stay in a place that has been satisfying for me creatively and happy for me personally.

Having a professional theatre exist side-by-side with an academic department is challenging, not the least because everyone has two jobs. Their day job is teaching (or being a student) and their night job is being involved with the theatre, either on or off stage. While there have been some difficulties with budgets (never big enough) and staff (the hybrid model is not suitable for every personality type), the synergy between the theatre and the classroom that exists on the Carolina campus is an ideal one nonetheless. Students take classes from working professionals (who also have strong academic credentials) and then can see them at work in the theatre or in one of the many workrooms and shops that support all these creative endeavors.

The energy that comes with every visiting guest artist (be they from New York, Los Angeles, or Raleigh) and the strong collaborative spirit that pervades the hallways between and among stage managers, the people working on press and public relations, actors, costume and technical folks, sound and lighting engineers, playwrights and directors, box office personnel, and those working on the business side is in evidence on opening night, when we all get dressed up and celebrate "another opening; another show."

The pace of theatre life can be frenetic and quite consuming: one show opens while another is in rehearsal and two or three more are being designed and cast and the following season is in the planning stages. This means that keeping track of history is often not especially important in the moment, much less taking pictures of everyone involved. Despite these obstacles, this book is an attempt to provide a record of how PlayMakers Repertory

Company began and to document the many, many people involved in the company over the years. It is organized around the artistic directors that have led it, with evocative essays written by Gregory Kable, Cecelia Moore, Adam Versényi, and Vivienne Benesch, all of whom have worked hard to be accurate and provide aesthetic context. The appendices contain a record of PRC productions, faculty members in the department of Dramatic Art, managing directors, and the 431 MFA degrees awarded since that first degree was conferred—coincidental with PRC's beginnings. I also want to thank Rosalie Preston for invaluable assistance with images, together with Linda Jacobson and Robert G. Anthony, Jr. in the North Carolina Collection in Wilson Library; Jamie Strickland (the amazing administrative manager in the Department of Dramatic Art since 2006) for tracking down details about personnel; David Adamson for chasing after cast members' names; Lynn Roundtree for excellent word-smithing; and Gordon Ferguson for being an expert (and patient) wizard with databases. I hope every name is spelled correctly and that everyone involved in the collaborative art called theatre feels acknowledged and celebrated—even if their names are not included.

When Milly Barranger was Chair, she encouraged me to consider writing a history of PRC following the model of Walter Spearman's book, *The Carolina Playmakers: The First Fifty Years*. Adam Versényi, the current Chair, helped make this dream a reality.

This book is dedicated to the nearly 2,000 cast members who appeared in 324 productions (to date) and to the countless members of running crews, students and professional staff working in the costume, scenery, and property workrooms, and the front-of house personnel who supported them—a figure that easily rises to two or three times that many. Because of all of you, the show indeed goes on.

PLAYMAKERS REPERTORY COMPANY

A HISTORY

INTRODUCTION

By Adam Versényi

This book traces the trajectory of the first fifty years of PlayMakers Repertory Company (PRC). As you will read in the pages that follow, when Tom Haas and Arthur Housman conceived of PlayMakers Repertory Company in 1975, they created a unique institution, a professional theatre company not only located on the campus of a major research university, but one embedded within UNC's Department of Dramatic Art. That combination of professional artistic achievement coupled with the highest quality theatrical training characterizes PlayMakers Repertory Company from its inception to the present day. Then as now, the core of the resident company—composed of faculty who are both teachers and practitioners—along with the graduate students in the Department's three MFA programs, is constantly supplemented by the best directors, designers, and performers working in the field today. Graduate students receive professional training during the day from teachers who become their collaborators at night both off and onstage. Undergraduates learn from faculty members who are constantly moving back and forth between the classroom and the stage, with the knowledge gained in one realm sparking creativity in the other.

This symbiotic relationship between PlayMakers Repertory Company (PRC) and the Department of Dramatic Art (DDA) builds upon a more than one-hundred-year legacy of theatrical activity at UNC-Chapel Hill. While the Department of Dramatic Art was formally established in 1936, UNC-Chapel Hill was the second university in the nation (after Carnegie Tech, now Carnegie Mellon University) to make theatrical training a part of its curriculum when Frederick Koch joined the University's English Department in 1918 to teach playwriting and dramatic literature. "Proff" Koch created the "American folk play" movement, turning out students that became luminaries of U.S. letters such as Thomas Wolfe and Paul Green. Building upon the work he had done at his previous institution, the University of North Dakota,

Paul Green Theatre, designed by Odell and Associates, opened 1977. Courtesy of the University of North Carolina at Chapel Hill Image Collection, North Carolina Collection Photographic Archives, UNC-Chapel Hill Library.

Koch also created The Carolina Playmakers, a company with a combination of university and community members that would eventually perform throughout the Southeast. In 1924 the University converted Smith Hall, a combination library and ballroom designed by the noted architect Alexander Jackson Davis, into Playmakers Theatre, creating the first dedicated theatre building on a state university campus in the nation. Playmakers Theatre, which housed the Department of Dramatic Art until it outgrew the building, was designated a National Historic Landmark in 1974 and is now known as Historic Playmakers Theatre.

As a public research university one of UNC-Chapel Hill's primary missions has always been to serve the state in which it is located, as well as the world beyond. PlayMakers Repertory Company, with its current outreach programs, builds upon the legacy of earlier Department of Dramatic Art programs. These include the Carolina Dramatic Association, founded in 1922 as a cooperative venture between Dramatic Art and the University Extension Division's Bureau of Community Drama, and the Institute of Outdoor Drama, founded as an affiliate of the Department in 1963 to promote outdoor dramas nationwide, including Paul Green's *The Lost Colony*, first performed in 1937.

When Tom Haas, PlayMakers Repertory Company's first Artistic Director, created PRC's precursor, the Graduate Acting Company, in 1975, he was

building upon UNC-Chapel Hill's legacy of combining theatrical production with theatrical training. Haas stated in 1979 that the new company's mission would be "to present and develop" U.S. writers, thereby cultivating the seeds sown by Proff Koch in 1918 when he launched the American folk play movement. When the Paul Green Theatre, PRC's main stage, opened in 1978 it was named for one of Koch's best-known students, the Pulitzer Prize winning playwright, UNC professor, and tireless advocate for civil liberties, Paul Green. The theatre, seating 498 (with an additional fifty standing-room only spaces) was designed by Odell and Associates at a cost of $1.6 million, and also contained the scene shop, a box office, and costume storage. In 1998 the Paul Green Theatre was incorporated into the Center for Dramatic Art, a new facility constructed at a cost of $10.8 million with $9.4 million coming from state appropriations and the rest from private funds. One of those private gifts came from Betty Kenan, whose $1 million gift to the Department created the 265–seat Elizabeth Price Kenan Theatre for student productions. The 55,000 square foot addition to the existing Paul Green Theatre added not only the new theatre, but a costume shop, a rehearsal hall, acting studios, traditional classrooms, and a new box office and reception area. By wrapping the new facility around the existing Paul Green Theatre, the Center for Dramatic Art brought all of the Department and the Company's operations under one roof

Architectural rendering of the Center for Dramatic Art, 1998; Architect: Graham Gund, Gund Partnership, Cambridge, Massachusetts. Courtesy of PRC.

for the first time. The complex was designed by Graham Gund, principal of Gund Partnership.

When Tom Haas left PlayMakers Repertory Company at the end of the 1979–1980 season, he was succeeded by David Rotenberg, who then served as Co-Artistic Director with Gregory Boyd in 1982, the same year that Milly S. Barranger became Chair of the Department of Dramatic Art and Producing Director of PlayMakers Repertory Company. During her tenure from 1982–1999, the relationship between the company and the department was further strengthened as the MFA programs were reduced to three: Acting, Costume Production, and Technical Production. By focusing on a few core programs, the Department was better able to enhance those students' experience with the professional company. Rotenberg and Boyd continued the focus on U.S. playwrights by producing several plays developed at the O'Neill Theater Center in Connecticut, through a long-standing relationship between the Center and the Department. Working with three different Artistic Directors, Barranger also established the Company's Artistic Director as the Head of the Professional Actor Training Program MFA when Rotenberg left in 1983 and Boyd became sole Artistic Director. This arrangement continued when Boyd left in 1985 and was succeeded by David Hammond. The Barranger-Hammond collaboration lasted until 1999 when Barranger retired. Together they further developed the close relationship between the Company and the Department, while building PlayMakers Repertory Company's national reputation.

With David Hammond's retirement from UNC-Chapel Hill in 2005, then Department Chair McKay Coble restructured the administration of PlayMakers Repertory Company, turning the Artistic Director, who had also been a full-time faculty member, into the new position of Producing Artistic Director with a secondary appointment as a faculty member associated with the MFA program in Acting. This new arrangement relieved the Producing Artistic Director of teaching responsibilities and the administrative responsibility of running the Professional Actor Training Program, thus enabling the incumbent to concentrate primarily on developing PRC and the necessary outreach activities beyond the bounds of the University. In 2006 Joseph Haj became the fifth person to lead the Company and the first to do so in the new configuration. As is detailed later in these pages, Haj fully grasped the possibilities inherent in his new position, expanding PRC's offerings on its main stage, adding a second stage season (and also a Summer Youth Conservatory), and bringing companies that specialized in devised work to Chapel Hill for residencies when the theatre was dark. (The latter unfolded over the course of six years funded by a grant from the Andrew W. Mellon Foundation).

The Summer Youth Conservatory (SYC) was initially directed by Haj's long-time collaborator in Los Angeles, Tom Quaintance, who also directed a number of productions for PRC. Since its inception in 2007 with the musical *Oliver!*, SYC has produced twelve productions with casts and stage crews of high school and middle school students, but directed, choreographed, and designed by professional artists. In classes early in the day, these young students then transition to rehearsal and production following the DDA/PRC working model and initiating the students into a professional mode of theatrical creation. Several of those students subsequently performed in or worked on PRC main stage productions. In this fashion SYC echoes the Junior Carolina Playmakers founded by DDA faculty member John Parker in 1938, as well as The Carolina Playmakers tours that introduced young people to theatre throughout the state.

In his new role as Producing Artistic Director Joseph Haj embodied the synergistic relationship between the Company and the Department, bringing it full circle. He joined the company as a graduate of the University's Professional Actor Training Program, who had performed in numerous PRC productions directed by David Hammond while he was a student. From 2006 to 2015, when he left to become the Artistic Director of the Guthrie Theater, Haj not only greatly increased PlayMakers artistic output, but also greatly broadened the artistic voices seen on the PlayMakers stage. This was accomplished largely by enacting a policy of creating seasons that were fifty percent written by and/or directed by women and people of color.

I became Chair of the Department in 2014. At that time former Chair McKay Coble and I helmed the committee that conducted a national search for a new Producing Artistic Director for PlayMakers, in the end selecting Vivienne Benesch as PRC's sixth leader, and the first woman to assume the post. Like Haj, when Benesch joined us she brought not only a prior relationship with PlayMakers, where she had previously directed, but also with the Department, where she had taught for a semester. Not only possessing extensive leadership experience from over a decade of work with the Chautauqua Theater Company, but also extensive teaching experience at the Juilliard School and New York University's theatre programs, Benesch came to Chapel Hill firmly invested in the combination of artistic excellence and quality theatrical training that has characterized PRC throughout its history.

As Chair and as Producing Artistic Director respectively, we share the conviction that the future of the arts in this country is, to a large extent, dependent upon university campuses—spaces where we have the freedom and the resources to expand the boundaries of our art form and also entertain the

Adam Versényi, 2016, on the Isle of Anglesey, off the coast of Wales. Photograph by Robin Kirk. Courtesy of Adam Versényi.

most pressing questions of the day. Since her arrival Vivienne Benesch has increased the panoply of artistic voices who have come to us as guest artists to work with the Company, while the Department has worked to broaden representation on its faculty. Currently in her fifth season as Producing Artistic Director, she has further built upon the legacy of producing new plays stretching back to Proff Koch with numerous world premieres, including two by Department of Dramatic Art alumni Bekah Brunstetter and Mike Wiley. She has also created PRC Mobile, a new initiative producing Shakespeare and other playwrights' work performed by graduate MFA Acting students, which has toured throughout North Carolina and into Virginia and echoes the Carolina Playmakers tours under Koch. Her focus on new work has also led to the creation of the Making Tracks Festival of New Plays (in collaboration with UNC's Process Series), and the inaugural Thomas Wolfe International Playwriting Prize (in collaboration with the Thomas Wolfe Society and the Thomas Wolfe Memorial).

In 2017 Joan H. Gillings announced a $12 million donation to the University of North Carolina at Chapel Hill, to be evenly split between PlayMakers and the Department. This single largest gift to the performing arts in the University's history re-named our facility the Joan H. Gillings Center for Dramatic Art—one made in recognition of the inextricable relationship between the Company and the Department that I have been tracing in this essay. Gillings' transformational gift well positions us to enter the second decade of the 21st century. We do so standing on the shoulders of those early Playmakers such as Thomas Wolfe, as well as more recent Playmakers such as Kathryn Meisle, Michael Cumpsty, Billy Crudup, and Sharon Lawrence, as well as the Department's alumni recognized by the University with Distinguished Alumni Awards including Mike Wiley, Alan Bergman, William Harris Brooks, Martha Nell Hardy, Mary Pope Osborne, George Grizzard, Richard Adler, Andy Griffith, Shepperd Strudwick, and Paul Green.

The last few productions of PlayMakers' 2019–2020 season—and the entirety of its 2020–2021 season—have been indelibly marked by the COVID-19 pandemic. Live productions have been eliminated and we have become engaged with new forms of creative expression as we seek to connect with our audience via the virtual world. No one knows precisely when the pandemic will end but as the pages you are about to read demonstrate, PlayMakers Repertory Company, in partnership with the Department of Dramatic Art, will go on. We will continue to grow artistically, to train the nation's future theatre artists, and to provide a platform for innovation, investigation, and discovery. Here's to the next fifty years!

ADAM VERSÉNYI, a dramaturg and translator, is author of *Theatre of Sabina Berman: The Agony of Ecstasy and Other Plays*; *Ramón Griffero: Your Desires in Fragments and Other Plays*; and the forthcoming translation of Griffero's *The Dramaturgy of Space*. In addition to being Chair of the Department of Dramatic Art from 2014–present, he was Chair of the Curriculum in International and Areas Studies (now Global Studies) from 2004–2009.

IN THE BEGINNING │ TOM HAAS

By Bobbi Owen

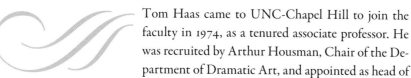Tom Haas came to UNC-Chapel Hill to join the faculty in 1974, as a tenured associate professor. He was recruited by Arthur Housman, Chair of the Department of Dramatic Art, and appointed as head of the newly created MFA degree programs in acting and directing. He came to Chapel Hill from New Haven, Connecticut where he had been a member of the faculty at the Yale University School of Drama and where he also led the acting and directing programs. Part of the appeal of moving to Chapel Hill for this single parent was creating a home for his two young sons, Campbell and Colin. Haas received his undergraduate education at Montclair State College and earned a master's degree at Cornell University and a Ph.D. from the University of Wisconsin-Madison. With these academic qualifications, he also brought teaching experience, having served on the faculty at both Queens College and Emerson College before joining the Yale University School of Drama in 1970. He also had directing credentials. Haas was co-founder, with Gibbs Murray, of the Weathervane Theater in 1966, a summer stock theater in Whitefield, New Hampshire, where he remained artistic director for over twenty-five years (and where he provided summer stock experience to numerous faculty members and students from UNC-Chapel Hill). He had directed *Operation Sidewinder* by Sam Shepard at Williamstown Theater Festival (with Michael Henry, Linda Gulder, and Sam Waterston) and Shakespeare's *Hamlet* at the New York Shakespeare Festival (with Rip Torn and Tammy Grimes).

Bobbi Owen, with both graduate and undergraduate degrees from the University of Wisconsin-Madison, joined the faculty at the same time as an assistant professor. She had been recruited to head the newly created MFA degree program in costume design.

The Department of Dramatic Art was undergoing many changes at that time and additional faculty members were necessary. New MFA degrees in acting, costume design, directing, lighting design, playwriting, scene design,

and technical direction had recently been authorized by the University of North Carolina System. The inaugural group of students had been recruited in 1973 and were already in place. Nineteen MFA degrees were awarded in at Commencement in May 1975. The BFA degree was eliminated and the BA degree, considered most appropriate in a liberal arts setting in a growing research university, was reconfigured. The MA degree as well as the PhD (a joint program with the Department of Comparative Literature) were in the process of being phased out.

There were also new facilities. The Department of Dramatic Art and the costume shop had moved the previous year into Graham Memorial, which became available when the Frank Porter Graham Student Union opened in 1969. Graham Memorial also had space for offices for faculty members, classrooms, and rehearsals as well as a small performance space on the lower level. The scene shop remained in Caldwell Annex, a World War II-era Company Barracks building (a number of which were used by the University to expand its physical plant). Judy Clark, who had been the administrative manager for several years, was recruited away by the Department of Athletics, and Jewell Dobbins was hired to replace her. That hiring proved to be a brilliant one, because the Rutherfordton, NC native was especially adept at organization and balancing a variety of needs and personalities. She "ran" the Department of Dramatic Art from 1976 until her retirement in 1992.

"Theatre / Carolina" logo, 1975–1976. Used at that time for both Carolina Playmakers and PlayMakers Repertory Company productions. Courtesy of PRC.

Tom Haas arrived to find an ambitious production schedule in the Department, with the Carolina Playmakers staging performances in the Koch Memorial Theatre (familiarly known as the Forest Theatre), Playmakers Theatre (subsequently referred to as Historic Playmakers Theatre), and in Graham Memorial. Students, both graduate and undergraduate, performed an equally ambitious schedule through the Laboratory Theatre (later called the LAB! Theatre) mainly in a black box theatre on the lower level of Graham Memorial. Many of the roles in Carolina Playmakers productions were performed by members of the community, leaving few opportunities for students. The production calendar for 1974–1975 had already been set and was followed, beginning with the musical *Hair* in the Forest Theatre in September 1974 and ending with *The Time of Your Life* in Playmakers Theatre in April 1975. That same spring, Haas directed *Henrik Ibsen's Peer Gynt Show*, which was written by Tom Haas and Philip Persinger, a graduate student in playwriting. It was performed in the Graham Memorial Lounge by the "Graduate Acting Company," the precursor of Playmakers Repertory Company.

With support from Arthur Housman, Tom Haas planned a production schedule for 1975–1976 that focused on the graduate students, giving them opportunities to act and direct in Graham Memorial. Haas named the large open space on the main floor of the old student union "The Graham Memorial Lounge Theatre." Other student productions (featuring both graduate and undergraduate students) and the Lab Theatre used the black box theatre on the lower level. The Carolina Playmakers continued with their accustomed production schedule, produced in The Forest Theatre and at Playmakers Theatre. What began as the Graduate Acting Company officially became "Playmakers

The Mad Dog Blues,
1975–1976. Poster.
Graphic by Frank
Holyfield. Courtesy of
the University of North
Carolina at Chapel Hill
Special Collection:
Posters from the
Department of
Dramatic Art, North
Carolina Collection,
UNC-Chapel Hill
Library.

Repertory Company" which was generally referred to as PRC (the capital M
in PlayMakers first came into use in 1983).

In the 1975–1976 academic year, the program and poster for *The Mad Dog
Blues* by Sam Shepard contained a visible announcement in the upper right
hand corner, that it was the "Professional PRC Debut." It ran from October 23
to November 2, 1975 in the Graham Memorial Lounge Theatre. Other productions for PRC that fall included *Isadora Duncan Sleeps with the Russian Navy*

by Jeff Wanshel, *Hot Grog* by Jim Wann and Bland Simpson (co-produced with Peg Leg Productions and performed at The Ranch House restaurant on Airport Road), and Philip Barrie's *Holiday*. *Hot Grog* was the first of several collaborations with members of the Red Clay Ramblers. The casts included professional actors (not all of whom were students) with some of them paid on Actor's Equity guest artist contracts.

In March 1976, "Playmakers Repertory Company" produced Paul Green and Kurt Weill's *Johnny Johnson* in Playmakers Theatre. The program for *Johnny Johnson* included the following staff list of PLAYMAKERS REPERTORY COMPANY: Tom Haas, Artistic Director; Joseph Coleman, Managing Director, Joe Simmons, Business Manager, and V. Cullum Rogers, Dramaturg. The cast, crew, and members of the production team, were all students (mainly graduate students) and faculty members.

All productions in the Fall 1976 Semester were under the aegis of the Carolina Playmakers, although PRC did tour *Poe and the House of Usher* by Joseph Coleman and Tom Haas to public schools in Murphey, Asheville, Gastonia, Boone, Burnsville, West Jefferson, and Pittsboro, in association with the North Carolina Department of Public Instruction.

On January 25, 1977, *The Crucible* by Arthur Miller opened in Playmakers Theatre. It marked the beginning of a formal relationship with LORT (the League of Resident Theatres). LORT is the primary US administrator for not-for-profit theatres, overseeing the collective bargaining agreements with Actors' Equity Association (AEA), the Stage Directors and Choreographers Society (SDC), and United Scenic Artists (USA). Tom Haas came to UNC-Chapel Hill already a member of SDC, and in December 1975 Bobbi Owen became a member of USA. Contracts for actors were arranged via LORT for the first time, a relationship that continues to this day. Members of the Equity Acting Company for the Spring 1977 season were Flair Bogan, Darrie Lawrence, John Morrow, William Preston, Frank Raiter, Ann Shepherd, and Shepperd Strudwick; the other members of the professional company were Cigdem Onat, Candace Burnett, Gordon Ferguson, Brian Keeler, Mina Penland, Mark Phialas, and Richard Ussery.

The program for *The Crucible* contained a page-long "Welcome to Playmakers Repertory Company's Spring, 1977 Season" essay by Tom Haas, acknowledging how much growth had occurred since the idea for a company was conceived in spring 1975. He placed an emphasis on creating "... a theatrical excitement provoking reflection, thought, emotion or laughter, embracing a wide but distinctive repertoire of plays: *New Plays* which explore aspects of our immediate moment of history; those *Bedrock American Plays* which constitute our uniquely American theatrical tradition; and finally, those plays from a *Universal Repertory* which still speak compellingly ... "

The Crucible, 1976–1977. *Left to right*: Jule Ferguson Selbo as Mary Warren, Patricia Slover (in bed) as Betty Parris, Frank Raiter as Reverend Samuel Parris, Esther Tate as Tituba, Brian Keeler as Reverend John Hale, Mina Penland Keeler as Mrs. Ann Putnam, Mark Phialas as Thomas Putnam. Costume Design by Nancy J. Woodfield, Set and Lighting Design by David M. Glenn. Courtesy of the University of North Carolina at Chapel Hill Image Collection, Dramatic Art Department Collection, North Carolina Collection Photographic Archives, UNC–Chapel Hill Library.

All's Well that Ends Well, 1976–1977. *Left to right*: Cigdem Onat as Helena, Brian Keeler as Bertram, Gordon Ferguson as Lavatch, Joe Simmons (aka Joseph Cole) as Parolles. Costume Design by Bobbi Owen, Set Design by Rick Pike, Lighting Design by David J. Lockner. Helena's costume made by Judy Adamson. Courtesy of PRC.

Haas also made a strong commitment to the concept of a company comprising artists working on stage and the ones working behind the scenes. The artistic focus for Playmakers Repertory Company under Tom Haas's artistic leadership remained the same throughout his tenure. It had three elements, as he wrote for the inside front cover of the *Of Mice and Men* playbill in October 1979:

1. To present works from the American repertory;
2. To develop new plays by American writers;
3. To re-view the classics from an American experience.

During the following four years, Tom Haas maintained this vision. He developed seasons of professional productions with an emphasis on American plays performed by company members, professional actors, and students from the MFA Graduate Training program, turning Playmakers Repertory Company ". . . from an idea into a reality." Together, Chair Arthur Housman and Artistic Director Tom Haas merged the educational mission of the Department of Dramatic Art with the artistic vision of Playmakers Repertory Company. Tom Haas stated their vision in eloquent terms in the October/November 1978 playbill for *Dracula, The Vampire King*: "Many of our artists are leaders in their professions—actors, directors, designers; others are just beginning their professional lives—students from the Department of Dramatic Art. This happy mixture of professionals and students is a joining together of the great tradition of American theatre with the great University of North Carolina at Chapel Hill. PRC believes the training of the student is a major responsibility and brings that student from the classroom to work side by side with the experienced artist creating the production. Thus, the young and passionate energies and dreams of the student meet the discipline, standards, and dreams of the experienced artist creating a professional theatre striving toward excellence on a university campus."

The Paul Green Theatre opened on September 29, 1978 with a performance of *Native Son* by Paul Green and Richard Wright, author of the novel on which the play was based. The play was written in Chapel Hill in late 1940 and early 1941 but not performed there until thirty-seven years later although

Once in a Lifetime, 1976–1977. Costume Design by Bobbi Owen for Darrie Lawrence as May. Courtesy of Bobbi Owen.

PRC logo, used from 1977 to 1983. Courtesy of PRC.

Equus, 1977–1978. Set Design by David M. Glenn. Courtesy of David Adamson.

it was performed in Broadway's St. James Theatre from March 24 through June 28, 1941. *Native Son* was a production of the Department of Dramatic Art and was directed by Lee R. Yopp who had been managing director of the Bucks County Playhouse in New Hope, Pennsylvania from 1967 to 1973, and who became director of the nearby Fort Bragg Playhouse in 1974 (where he remained until 1993). Carolina undergraduate Gordon Cureton played the role of Bigger Thomas. (Cureton would receive his MFA in acting in 1981.)

For the first few years, the Paul Green Theatre was used for Department of Dramatic Art productions while PRC performed in the Graham Memorial Lounge Theatre and at Playmakers Theatre on Cameron Avenue. When *Threads* by Jonathan Bolt opened on November 8, 1978, the Paul Green Theatre became the primary performance space for PRC.

During his tenure as Artistic Director Tom Haas had several *firsts*:

- He hired actors for single performances and when appropriate retained them as company members. Frank Raiter and Darrie Lawrence followed by Michael Lipton, came to Chapel Hill from New York and helped form the core of the professional acting company. They performed alongside graduate students and faculty members, many of whom had professional experience (including Professor Patricia Barnett);

- He brought a professional stage manager, Errol Selsby, to Chapel Hill standardizing back stage as well as on-stage activity;
- He introduced audiences to the scenery and costumes of Steve Rubin, an MFA degree recipient from the Yale University School of Drama, who designed in major regional theatres, as the first-ever guest designer, when the production of *Hamlet* starring Ray Wise in the lead role, opened in January 1978;
- He varied the size of production, some of which had small casts and others large ones. For *Once in a Lifetime* he had 56 performers on stage—at one time—in the original Playmakers Theatre (now Historic Playmakers Theatre), a number yet to be exceeded;
- He hired Mary Gallagher as director of *Uncommon Women and Others* by Wendy Wasserstein in spring 1978. She became the first woman to direct for PRC
- He produced and directed the first musical for PRC, *Johnny Johnson,* in 1975–1976 season, followed four years later by *Side by Side by Sondheim* in November 1979.

Ah, Wilderness!, 1977–1978. *Left to right:* Teresa Westbrook as Mildred, Campbell Haas as Tommy, Frank Raiter as Nat Miller (standing), Joy Duncan as Serving Girl, John Daggan as Richard, Dorothy Lancaster as Lily Miller, Brian McNally as Arthur, and Barbara Sohmers as Essie. Costume Design by Bobbi Owen, Set and Lighting Design by David M. Glenn. Costumes made by Judy Adamson. Photograph by Bobbi Owen.

Long Day's Journey into Night, 1978–1979. Frank Raiter as James Tyrone and Ann Shepherd as Mary Cavan Tyrone. Costume Design by Bobbi Owen; Set and Lighting Design by David M. Glenn. Photograph by Bobbi Owen.

Importantly, he obtained recognition for Playmakers Repertory Company from the national theatre community when TCG (Theatre Communications Group) recognized PRC in the fall of 1976 and when the National Endowment for the Arts awarded a grant to the Company in January 1977. Both Tom Haas and Arthur Housman understood that while they had planted "the seeds of a viable and active theatre" it was also necessary to look to ". . . our audience, our benefactors, and our patrons—for your continued recognition, encouragement, and support . . ." for Playmakers Repertory Company to prosper and serve the community, as they wrote together in the announcement of PRC's second season in early 1977.

Tom Haas remained artistic director through the 1979–1980 season, after which he left Chapel Hill to become the artistic director of the Indiana Repertory Theatre in Indianapolis, Indiana. He directed a total of sixteen productions for PRC beginning with *Johnny Johnson* in 1975 and ending with *No Time for Comedy*. Highlights include *Ah, Wilderness!*, *Sherman the Peacemaker* (written by James Reston, Jr. who was on the faculty of the Department of English at that time), *Long Day's Journey into Night*, and *Hamlet*. He

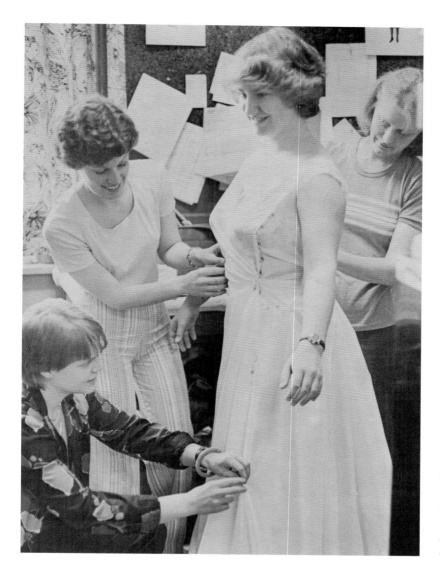

Costume fitting in the Graham Memorial Costume Shop, 1980–1981. *Left to right*: Bobbi Owen, Carol Vick, Michael Pridgen (fit model), and Judy Adamson. Courtesy of PRC.

adapted plays including *Dracula, The Vampire King* for PRC, and *A Christmas Carol* for the Department of Dramatic Art.

BOBBI OWEN is the author of several books and hundreds of articles about theatrical designers including *The Designs of William Ivey Long, Broadway Design Roster: Designers and Their Credits,* and *The Designs of Willa Kim. Edges of Time*, in the 2020–2021 season, is the 55th PRC production for which she has designed costumes.

NEW VOICES AND BIG IDEAS

DAVID ROTENBERG AND GREGORY BOYD

By Cecelia Moore

 Artistic director Tom Haas had selected the PRC productions for 1980–1981 before his departure. Department Chair Arthur Housman oversaw the season, which included classics and a new work that emerged from the Department's long partnership with the National Playwrights' Conference of the Eugene O'Neill Memorial Theatre Center. Housman also invited guest artists to direct a production as a way of auditioning them for the job of PRC artistic director. David Rotenberg, Housman's ultimate choice, directed the second production of the season, *Mrs. Warren's Profession* by George Bernard Shaw; as well as a new work by John Pielmeier, *Agnes of God*. Pielmeier's play had received a staged reading at the Eugene O'Neill Theater Center in 1979 followed by a production at the Humana Festival at Actors Theatre of Louisville in 1980. The PRC production in 1981, with a new cast featuring guest artists Elizabeth Franz and Jill Larson and faculty member Patricia Barnett, was one of a handful of regional theatre productions for the play before it went to Broadway in 1982.

At that time, PRC was continuing to build audience and benefactor support, as reported by Priscilla Bratcher, Director of Audience Development, in the March 1981 playbill for *The Fourposter*. The number of subscribers increased, "from 62% to 72% of capacity," she reported, reaffirming that the company had gained a good measure of local recognition and support in its first four years. There were performances for area school groups, which included post-performance discussions and actor visits to the classroom, a speaker's bureau, and a growing volunteer organization. The season concluded with a production of Shakespeare's *A Midsummer Night's Dream*, and the announcement that David Rotenberg would become Visiting Artistic Director of PRC in the fall of 1981.

Above: David Rotenberg. Courtesy of PRC.

Right: *Agnes of God*, 1980–1981. *Left to right*: Patricia Barnett as Mother Miriam Ruth and Jill Larson as Agnes. Costume Design by Bobbi Owen, Set and Lighting Design by David M. Glenn. Photograph by Bobbi Owen.

David Rotenberg came to Chapel Hill from the Williamstown Theatre Festival in Massachusetts. He was born in Toronto, Canada, and held a BA from the University of Toronto and an MFA in directing from the Yale University School of Drama. He had directed at various theatres in Canada and the United States, including productions Off-Broadway and with the Equity theatres at Princeton and Yale. Rotenberg, who was also a Visiting Associate Professor in the Department of Dramatic Art, directed four of the six productions for the 1981–1982 season, including the season opener, *The Front Page* by Ben Hecht and Charles MacArthur. "The finest example of American theatrical farce," Rotenberg noted in the playbill for this show. "The only thing which limits its number of revivals is its extraordinarily large cast." He noted that Playmakers could stage it because of its large company made up of students and faculty, augmented by guest artists. Rotenberg continued PRC's commitment to new work as well that year, bringing playwright Robert Litz to be in residence in Chapel Hill for the world premiere of his play, *Mobile Hymn*.

Above: *The Front Page*, 1981–1982. *Left to right*: Ivar Brogger as Hildy Johnson, Gregory Boyd as McCue of City Press, Ann Shepherd as Mrs. Grant, Emile Trimble as Peggy Grant. Costume Design by Bobbi Owen, Set Design by David M. Glenn, Lighting Design by Norman Coates. Photograph by Bobbi Owen.

Twelfth Night, 1981–1982. J. Smith Cameron as Viola, David Romero as Fabian, Richard Pait as Antonio, Paul Miles as Sir Andrew Aguecheek, Hamilton Gillett as Sir Toby Belch. Costume Design by Bobbi Owen, Set Design by Linwood Taylor, Lighting Design by Norman Coates. Photograph by Bobbi Owen.

Gregory Boyd.
Courtesy of PRC.

Gregory Boyd also came to Chapel Hill in 1981, as Associate Artistic Director for Playmakers and Visiting Associate Professor of Dramatic Art. Boyd was a graduate of the University of California at Berkeley and received an MFA in directing from Carnegie Mellon University. He had worked with David Rotenberg at the Williamstown Theatre Festival. In addition to his work at Williamstown, he had directed regional opera and taught at Carnegie Mellon and at Williams College. Boyd directed two PRC productions in the 1981–1982 season: *The Glass Menagerie* by Tennessee Williams and *Angel Street* by Patrick Hamilton.

In the fall of 1982, after a national search, the University selected Milly S. Barranger to succeed Arthur Housman as Chair of the Department of Dramatic Art. She came from Tulane University in New Orleans, where she had led their Department of Theatre and Speech and had helped to restructure the undergraduate theatre major. She had also been a visiting professor or a visiting scholar at the University of Tennessee-Knoxville, the Yale University School of Drama, and the University of Tulsa. In addition, she was active with university theatre associations on the national level and had written two well-received textbooks, including *Theatre: A Way of Seeing*—which is currently in its seventh edition.

Barranger also became Producing Director at PRC, which signaled her intention to strengthen the relationship between the professional theatre and academic programs. David Rotenberg and Gregory Boyd served as PRC co-artistic directors during that season while the latter also led the department's

Life on the Mississippi,
1982–1983. The Red
Clay Ramblers, *Left to
right*: Phillip Michael
Craver, Clay Buckner,
Jim Watson, Chris
Frank, Jack Herrick,
Tommy Thompson.
Costume Design by
Bobbi Owen, Set De-
sign by Linwood Taylor,
Lighting Design by
Norman Coates. Photo-
graph by Bobbi Owen.

MFA acting program. Between 1981 and 1985, PRC demonstrated the promise of what a residential professional company and a graduate training program could do working together. Rotenberg and Boyd planned ambitious produc-tions that were a mix of new works and classics, while Milly Barranger guided refinements to the MFA programs in acting, costume production, and techni-cal production. (In the process, the other MFA programs, which had smaller enrollments, were eliminated.) She also increased efforts to recruit donors and volunteers, and to secure additional support from the University.

The 1982–1983 season opened with PRC's first full-scale musical, a collabo-ration with the Red Clay Ramblers, the band with which the company had co-produced *Hot Grog* in 1975. This new show, *Life on the Mississippi*, based on the memoirs of Mark Twain, was written by band members Bland Simpson and Tommy Thompson. The production featured a nineteen-person cast of professional artists, graduate students, and undergraduates. With costume de-sign by Bobbi Owen and scenic design by Linwood Taylor, the company's resi-dent designers and faculty members, the show turned the Paul Green Theatre stage into a "majestic, gingerbread-trimmed" steamboat, according to Charles Horton, drama critic for the *Chapel Hill News*. In his opinion, *Life on the Mississippi* was "the handsomest and most theatrically-successful production" staged by PlayMakers to that point.

The Greeks, 1982–1983.
Left to right: Sharon
Lawrence as Electra,
Henry Hoffman as
Orestes, Michael
Cumpsty as Pylades.
Costume Design by
Bobbi Owen, Set
Design by Peter David
Gould, Lighting Design
by Norman Coates.
Photograph by Bobbi
Owen.

That same season, PRC staged *The Greeks*, a re-telling of the Trojan War based on the works of Homer and the Greek tragedies. This was the company's first rotating repertory production. Divided into two parts with a cast of forty and staged on successive evenings, *The Greeks* was a reflection on the Vietnam War and the conflicted feelings of Americans in its aftermath. In the playbill, Gregory Boyd explained that a project of this scope showed how a professional company—with students in "a new and rigorous professional training program"—could "put its theories and practices to the test of living theatre."

The Greeks also showcased the promise of the actor training program at Chapel Hill. Making their PRC debuts in the cast were MFA students Michael Cumpsty, Herman LaVern Jones, and Kathryn Meisle, as well as a promising undergraduate, Sharon Lawrence. Each of these students went on to successful acting careers. In Jones' case, acting eventually led to teaching,

Pygmalion, 1982–1983. Douglas Johnson as Henry Higgins and Kathryn Meisle as Eliza Doolittle. Costume Design by Bobbi Owen, Set Design by Linwood Taylor, Lighting Design by Norman Coates. Costume for Eliza made by Suzanne Y. Wilkins. Photograph by Bobbi Owen.

and to producing and directing in regional theatre, including with the National Black Theatre Festival.

That season ended with a production of *Pygmalion* directed by Gregory Boyd with MFA student Kathryn Meisle as Eliza Doolittle. Douglas Johnson, who played Henry Higgins, would return to direct additional productions in the following three seasons often featuring graduate students.

David Rotenberg left PRC in Spring 1983 for New York City, which beckoned with more opportunities for him to direct. He had directed eight Play-Makers productions in all, including the Simpson-Thompson musical *Life on the Mississippi*, and helped to lay the groundwork for the company's growth. For 1983–1984, Boyd served as Artistic Director and launched "PlayFest," a rotating repertory of three productions running simultaneously in the Paul Green Theatre. The first of these, PlayFest '84, included the Oscar Wilde classic *The Importance of Being Earnest*, Tom Stoppard's *Travesties*, and an innovative musical adaptation of Bram Stoker's famous novel, *Dracula: A Musical Nightmare*. *Dracula* featured Joe Spano, one of the stars of the hit

TV show "Hill Street Blues." (Boyd and Spano had worked together at the Berkeley Rep.) *Dracula* was written by Douglas Johnson with music by John Aschenbrenner. The premiere in Chapel Hill led to a successful run for the show the following summer—with the full cast and creative team intact—at the Alcazar Theatre in San Francisco.

The *Playbill* for the opening production of the 1983–1984 season, William Shakespeare's *As You Like It,* introduced a new look for all promotional materials including the logo. A capital M was inserted into the word "PlayMakers," to further distinguish the professional repertory company from the older "Carolina Playmakers" group, which was not a professional endeavor.

The 1984–1985 season, the company's ninth, was its most ambitious yet. The schedule included two contemporary pieces, two world premieres, two classics, and PlayFest '85. The first of the premieres was a new musical by Jerry Colker and Michael Rupert, *Three Guys Naked from the Waist Down,* which was a pre-Off-Broadway tryout. David Rotenberg returned to direct the second premiere, *The Last Song of John Proffit,* by Tommy Thompson of the Red Clay Ramblers. This production has the distinction of being the last Play-Makers Repertory Company production staged in Historic Playmakers Theatre. In addition, the production of *Our Town* by Thornton Wilder featured UNC-Chapel Hill alumnus and Emmy-winning daytime television actor James Pritchett as the Stage Manager; while the closing production of *Cyrano* starred Michael Cumpsty in the lead—his last role while he was a graduate student in the University's professional actor training program.

The company's ninth season was also its most successful to date, in terms of income, audience growth, and artistic recognition. Attendance for PRC shows reached 52,000, more than 90% of the capacity of the Paul Green Theatre. On one weekend in October of 1984, more than 4,000 audience members had attended one of three productions—a Department of Dramatic Art performance of *An Evening With Tennessee Williams*, a student Lab Theatre double bill of *The Idiot Box* and *Altered Mates*, or PRC's *She Stoops to Conquer*, a sold-out run. This kind of success paralleled PRC's participation in the development of national resident and educational theatre scenes. *Dracula* had travelled from Chapel Hill for a successful run in San Francisco; *Three Guys Naked from the Waist Down* had opened Off-Broadway and was still running; while the *Last Song of John Proffit* was set for an upcoming video production (through a collaboration with the UNC Center for Public Television).

The conclusion of the 1984–1985 season brought more changes. Gregory Boyd departed to become artistic director of StageWest in Springfield, Massachusetts, while the company's Producing Director, Robert W. Tolan, de-

Our Town, 1984–1985. James Pritchett as the Stage Manager. Costume Design by Bobbi Owen, Set Design by Linwood Taylor, Lighting Design by Charles Catotti. Photograph by Bobbi Owen.

parted to lead Heritage Artists, Ltd. at the Cohoes, New York Music Hall. (Milly Barranger became Executive Producer when Robert Tolan was appointed Producing Director in the fall of 1983.) By the time of his departure, Boyd had directed twelve PRC productions, led the professional actor training program, and helped to shape the company's reputation for staging ambitious productions.

He had quickly earned a reputation in Chapel Hill for "directing provocative renditions of traditional texts," as *Daily Tar Heel* arts editor (and future *New York Times* reporter) Frank Bruni noted in a profile of Boyd in April 1985. From his first PRC production of Chekhov's *Three Sisters* in 1982 to his final production of *Cyrano de Bergerac* in 1985, Boyd's direction was based on what he called "compelling juxtapositions." These might contrast "costume with character, prop with costume, set with action, music with set" to produce a "startling image indigenous to a Boyd production." His work had been both denounced and praised by audiences and critics, but overall it brought more favorable attention to the company and the academic programs.

Cyrano de Bergerac, 1984–1985. Front row (*left to right*): Kieran Connolly (kneeling) as Ligniere, Kathryn Meisle as Roxane, Robin Dorff as a Cadet, David Adamson as Le Bret. Back row (*left to right*): Bill Goulet as Comte de Guiche, Steve Maler (partially obscured) as a Musketeer, Peter Hertsgaard as Christian de Neuvilette, David Gottlieb as comte de Valvert, John Feltch as Cuigy, William Meisle as Rageneau. Costume Design by Bobbi Owen, Set Design by Linwood Taylor, Lighting Design by Robert Jared. Photograph by Bobbi Owen.

Repertory Company

With a new artistic director about to come on board in 1985, PRC Executive Producer Milly Barranger would capitalize on these years of experimentation to build an even stronger artistic and financial structure for PlayMakers Repertory Company and its connection to the academic programs in the Department of Dramatic Art.

Left: Milly S. Barranger. Courtesy of Milly S. Barranger.

Right: PRC logo, used from 1983 to 1988 (the capital "M" is inserted into "PlayMakers" for the first time). Courtesy of PRC.

CECELIA MOORE is the former University Historian for the University of North Carolina at Chapel Hill. She holds an MA in public history from North Carolina State University, and a PhD in history from UNC-Chapel Hill. She is the author of *The Federal Theatre Project in the American South: The Carolina Playmakers and the Quest for American Drama* and co-author of *UNC A to Z: What Every Tar Heel Needs to Know about the First State University*. She was the director of development for PlayMakers Repertory Company and the Department of Dramatic Art from 1995 to 1999.

NEW HORIZONS | MILLY S. BARRANGER AND DAVID HAMMOND

By Gregory Kable

Dr. Milly S. Barranger served as PRC Executive Director (her title varied) from 1982 to 1999, while also serving as the Chair for the Department of Dramatic Art. Her organizational acumen, deft leadership, and consistent vision would guide the company through seventeen seasons and more than one hundred productions. David Hammond, already notable for a distinguished national and regional career in theatre, joined the faculty and company in the role of Artistic Director in 1985, with Barranger continuing as departmental Chair and with the title of Producing Director for PlayMakers.

Barranger and Hammond ushered in a vivid chapter in the history of Play-Makers. Seasons would grow both in scope and scale, the company's visibility and national profile enjoyed steady growth, and most important of all, devoted fund raising efforts—with a themed Playmakers Ball as an annual highlight—would result in Barranger's long-held goal of establishing a central campus base for the disparate parts of the department and company. Breaking ground in 1996, the Center for Dramatic Art (CDA) opened in 1998, being renamed The Joan H. Gillings Center for Dramatic Art in 2017.

The 55,000 square foot complex abutting the existing Paul Green The-atre provided the necessary space for academic and studio classrooms, and faculty offices, supporting the department's educational role, as well as the public lobbies, rehearsal hall, dressing and green rooms, additional shop space and technical offices, and particularly a dedicated storage facility for a massive costume collection, required by an efficient production wing. A second performance venue, the intimate Elizabeth Price Kenan Theatre, was opened as a state-of-the-art space for undergraduate production within the building itself, complementing continued student use of Historic Playmakers Theatre which remained as sought-after and prolific as ever. That space was used for

David Hammond, on the partially completed set for *Tartuffe*, 1992–1993. Costume and Set Design by Bill Clarke, Lighting Design by Mary Louise Geiger. Courtesy of PRC.

Look Homeward, Angel, 1986–1987. Lance Guest as Eugene Gant and Betsy Friday as Laura James. Costume Design by Bobbi Owen, Set Design by Linwood Taylor, Lighting Design by Robert Wierzel. Courtesy of PRC.

faculty-led productions, those of the departmentally-affiliated LAB! Theatre, and hosting other campus organizations such as Pauper Players, Company Carolina, and an array of campus a cappella groups.

The synergy between the educational and creative work within the CDA, and its benefit to the University as a whole, was palpable from the start and remains so today. Reflecting on the company's tenth anniversary Professor Barranger noted in the playbill for *Look Homeward, Angel* how "our producing organization reflects at all levels (undergraduate and graduate, professional and non-professional) the combined missions of a professional theatre, an advanced training program, and an educational department."

A major part of Barranger's legacy is her persistence of vision in turning that dream into a reality. This fortitude combined with her administrative guidance of both the department and company, her championing by example and through mentoring for the advancement of women in the American Theatre, and the consistently high standards of her teaching and scholarship, led to her being celebrated as a 'woman of valor' on the occasion of her retirement. Under Milly Barranger's aegis, both Dramatic Art and PlayMakers found a single, prominent home.

Happily, the Barranger-Hammond leadership was as notable for continuity as for progress. Hammond crafted a statement of purpose which serves as a bridge between the company's distinguished past and its future:

> "The term 'playmaker' has roots in Elizabethan England, but it came into popular usage in the United States with the emergence, early in the twentieth century, of the American "folk drama"—a theatre that sprang from and spoke directly to the lives of its audience. This movement achieved its most influential voice with the founding of the Carolina Playmakers. Today, PlayMakers Repertory Company embraces its legacy of 'playmaking' with a three-fold mission:
>
> (1) to engage our community in an ongoing exploration of the nature and significance of theatre in contemporary life;
> (2) to investigate the theatrical event and the methods used for its realization in performance;
> (3) to nurture succeeding generations of artists and audiences to continue our work.

Between his first and final productions, Ostrovsky's Russian classic *The Storm* and Bernard Shaw's *Caesar and Cleopatra* two decades later, David Hammond would direct a record thirty-six productions over the span of twenty-one

PRC logo, used from 1989 to 1999. Courtesy of PRC.

Waiting for Godot, 1987–1988.
John Feltch as Vladimir and Tandy
Cronyn as Estragon. Costume Design by Laurel Clayson, Set Design
by Linwood Taylor, Lighting Design
by Robert Wierzel. Photograph by
Kevin Keister. Courtesy of PRC.

seasons. And that trio of injunctions would prove to be the touchstones and catalysts for advancing the repertory under his tenure.

Overall, season selections were broad and adventurous, and a representative sampling of Hammond's own productions proves just how dynamic this period was. The 1987–1988 showpiece of Eugene O'Neill's *Mourning Becomes Electra,* an epic trilogy transposing Greek Tragedy into America's Civil War era, was emblematic of the kind of ambition and daring undertaken by the evolving company. *The Nutcracker: A Play* based on the short story by E.T.A. Hoffmann, was one of several esteemed, high-profile productions Hammond would both adapt and direct for the PlayMakers stage (debuting in 1990, *The Nutcracker,* in particular, enjoyed popular revival over several holiday seasons).

Hammond began 2001–2002 with Moises Kaufman and the Tectonic Theatre's *The Laramie Project,* a brave, uncompromising work employing documentary theatre methods and advocating for gay dignity well before such compassion began passage toward a cultural norm, its power furthered by its deliberate bookending with a companion Hammond piece, Thornton Wilder's *Our Town* at season's end. Lastly, *The Tragedy of King Richard II* exemplified a cornerstone of Hammond's many strengths—his encyclopedic knowledge of, passion for, and theatrical fluency with Shakespeare.

The Nutcracker: A Play, 1989–1990, 1990–1991, 1991–1992, 1992–1993, 1996–1997, 1997–1998. Costume Design by McKay Coble for Susanna Rinehart as Mouserinks. (Eve Eaton appeared as Mouserinks in 1991–1992). Courtesy of McKay Coble.

The Nutcracker: A Play, 1989–1990. *Left to right*: Daniel Krell as the Mouse Prince, Aaron Carlos as the Prince, Lynn Passarella as Marie, and Susanna Rinehart as Mouserinks. Courtesy of PRC.

Many surrogate titles could be substituted for those above, equally indicative of Hammond's rare combination of rigorous intelligence and fluid staging. Indeed, Shakespeare would be a frequent source, with Hammond directing a total of nine of the plays from across the canon beginning with *Much Ado About Nothing* at the close of that inaugural 1985–1986 season, followed by *A Midsummer Night's Dream* the following year, and *Romeo and Juliet* in 1987–1988. Hammond's *The Taming of the Shrew* was featured in 1988–1989, and *Pericles* the season after. *Hamlet* was produced in 1992–1993, and *Othello* in 1995–1996. In 2001, *All's Well That Ends Well* concluded the 25th Anniversary season, prior to 2004–2005's aforementioned *Richard II*.

And productions ranging from Ketti Frings' dramatization of Thomas Wolfe's *Look Homeward, Angel;* Samuel Beckett's *Waiting for Godot;* Anton Chekhov's *The Cherry Orchard;* Moliere's *Tartuffe;* Frank Galati's adaptation of John Steinbeck's *The Grapes of Wrath;* Friedrich Durrenmatt's *The Visit;* Tom Stoppard's *Arcadia;* Stephen Sondheim and Hugh Wheeler's musicalization of an Ingmar Bergman film, *A Little Night Music;* Simon Bent's stage version of John Irving's novel *A Prayer for Owen Meany;* and the American premiere of Nick Stafford's *Luminosity*, would tell a similar tale. To the clear critical eye shared with Barranger, Hammond brought an actor-director's instinct for arresting action, a choreographic grace with physicality and movement, a seasoned showman's flair for storytelling, and an artist's commitment to championing truth.

Festival Stage designed by
Desmond Heeley, 1988.
Courtesy of PRC.

"All of our productions," Hammond reinforced in a program note, "are chosen in pursuit of our mission, investigating the nature and significance of theatre in contemporary life, exploring the potential of what can happen when a community assembles to participate in a shared experience of self-examination and reflection."

The Beggar's Opera, by John Gay, adapted and directed by David Hammond, was the final production in the 1987–1988 season. It was the initial production using a "festival stage" design, which was devised by the great scenic and costume designer Desmond Heeley, who had created a similar environment for the Stratford Shakespearean Festival in Stratford, Ontario. The stage space was juxtaposed to the wide entrance space (used by the audience). McKay Coble's set for *The Beggar's Opera*—and those for several years to come—was integrated into that stage configuration.

Many core company members and notable guest artists added to that growing community:

- Established directors, Evan Yionoulis, Andre Ernotte, Nagle Jackson, John Dillon, and Trezana Beverley, alternated with Broadway and television veterans Gene Saks, Jeffrey Hayden, and Joan Darling, and the masterful Hungarian director László Marton.
- Younger directors like Tazewell Thompson, John Rando, Bartlett Sher, Drew Barr, Loretta Greco, and Michael Sexton, and former undergraduates Michael Wilson and Ted Shaffner brought new perspectives and energies to the fold, as did company members Ray Dooley and DeDe Corvinus when they were tapped to direct.

From the Mississippi Delta, 1995–1996. Kimberly Hawthorne as Woman One, Crystal Laws Green as Woman Three, and Gwendolyn Mulamba as Woman Two. Costume Design by Maria E. Marrero, Set Design by Donald Eastman, Lighting Design by Ashley York Kennedy. Courtesy of PRC.

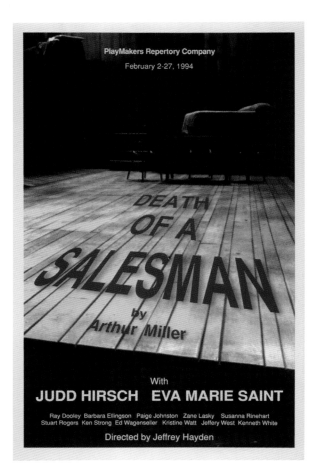

Death of a Salesman, 1993–1994, Poster. Costume Coordination by Sharon K. Campbell and Caryn Newman, Set Design by Sarah L. Lambert, Lighting Design by Mary Louise Geiger. Courtesy of PRC.

- Actress Tandy Cronyn made her PlayMakers debut in 1985–1986 with *Much Ado About Nothing,* making frequent returns over the next eighteen seasons.
- Kyle MacLachlan was Romeo in 1987–1988's *Romeo and Juliet.*
- Judd Hirsch and Eva Marie Saint co-starred in Arthur Miller's *Death of a Salesman* in 1993–1994, with Saint also playing a benefit performance of A.R. Gurney's poignant *Love Letters* alongside UNC-Chapel Hill alumnus George Grizzard.
- Ellen Burstyn, Matthew Broderick, and Polly Holliday headlined the cast of Horton Foote's *The Death of Papa* in 1996–1997.
- Lighting designers Robert Wierzel and Mary Louise Geiger, scenic and costume designer Russell Parkman, and scenic designer Narelle Sissons would make striking contributions over many seasons.

The Death of Papa, 1996–1997. *Left to right*: Ellen Burstyn as Mary Vaughn, Nikki Coleman-Andrews (standing) as Gertrude, Hallie Foote as Elizabeth Robedaux, Nicholas Shaw as Horace Robedaux, Jr., Matthew Broderick as Brother Vaughn, and Ray Virta as Horace Robedaux, Sr. Costume Design by McKay Coble, Set Design by Jeff Cowie, Lighting Design by Michael Lincoln. Costume for Elizabeth Robedaux made by Judy Adamson and for Mary Vaughn made by Erika Malos. Courtesy of PRC.

The Death of Papa, 1996–1997. Polly Holliday as Corella Davenport and Julie Fishell as Inez Kirby. Costume Design by McKay Coble, Set Design by Jeff Cowie, Lighting Design by Michael Lincoln. Costumes for Corella Davenport made by Lisa Davis. Courtesy of PRC.

Wit, 1999–2000.
Kathryn Hunter-
Williams as Susie
Monahan, R.N., B.S.N.
and Tandy Cronyn as
Dr. Vivian Bearing,
PhD. Costume Design
by Jennifer Reider,
Set Design by Narelle
Sissons, Lighting Design
by Mary Louise Geiger.
Courtesy of PRC.

- Company members (and faculty members) David Adamson, Jeffrey Blair Cornell, Ray Dooley, Julie Fishell, Kathryn Hunter-Williams, Gregory Kable, Michael Rolleri, Kenneth Strong, Craig Turner, and Adam Versényi, would all become long-standing faculty members and resident artists and staff during this period.
- Both subscribers and students were enriched by a pair of lively symposiums moderated by Hammond, one on theatre and censorship in North Carolina, the other featuring a panel of distinguished former Carolina Playmakers.
- Indicative of the company's abiding ambition, Mark Wing-Davey's visceral 2003–2004 *King Lear* played in both full-length and ninety-minute versions.
- Administrative support came from Ray Dooley, who served as Department Chair from 1999–2000 through the Fall of 2004, and from McKay Coble, who succeeded Dooley as Chair from Spring 2005 through 2013–2014. In addition, Phyllis Ryan, the department's Administrative Manager, devotedly served from 1997 to 2006.
- Support for production was provided by Production Managers, a new position that began with Tom Neville in 1987. He was followed by Jerry Genochio, Kenneth J. Lewis, and Jason T. Prichard among others; since 2006 Michael Rolleri has been Production Manager.

Ray Dooley on the set of
Master Class, 1997–1998. Set
Design by Donald Eastman.
Courtesy of PRC.

The Man Who Came to Dinner, 2001–2002. Alton
Fitzgerald as Beverly Carlton. Costume Design by
Patrick Holt, Set Design by Bill Clarke, Lighting
Design by Peter West. Courtesy of PRC.

- Further contributors were the many able Managing Directors including George Parides, Robert W. Tolan, Jonathan L. Giles, Margaret Hahn, Regina F. Lickteig, Mary Robin Wells, Zannie Giraud Voss, Donna Bost Heins, and Mary Lee Porterfield.

The sheer range and variety of these seminal seasons and respective talents speaks to one of the intentional virtues of the repertory system. As Hammond maintained in 2004, "We do not present a single 'type' of play . . . We hope that the only things our productions have in common with each other is quality." A questing spirit coupled with a commitment to aesthetic integrity were the hallmarks of the Barranger and Hammond years.

GREGORY KABLE has been a production dramaturg on nearly fifty PRC productions since 1997. He has covered the alphabet in two dozen directing projects ranging from Alan Ayckbourn through Tennessee Williams, and Georg Buchner to Lanford Wilson, including works by Strindberg, Sam Shepard, and Sondheim.

BEYOND BORDERS | JOSEPH HAJ

By Gregory Kable

 There's a familiar maxim in the theatre attributed to the seminal actor-director Konstantin Stanislavski: "Love the art in yourself, not yourself in the art," a reminder to remain humble in the face of a heady, uncertain profession. This ideal succinctly characterizes the tenure of Joseph Haj, who served as PlayMakers' fifth Artistic Director (redesignated Producing Artistic Director) for nine adventurous seasons from 2006 to 2015. As it will become readily apparent, Haj's appointment, by McKay Coble who was chair of the Department of Dramatic Art, was more truly a homecoming.

Joseph Haj's journey at Carolina began in fall 1985 as a graduate student in the Professional Actors Training Program. As part of that curriculum, he made his PlayMakers' debut as an ensemble member in the initial productions of the 1985–1986 season, Oliver Goldsmith's *She Stoops to Conquer* and *The Storm* by Alexander Ostrovsky. Cast in varied roles over the next few seasons, most notably as Mercutio in the 1987–1988 *Romeo and Juliet*, Haj continued the career of a working actor after graduation, including participation in the first renowned SITI Company production founded by experimentalists Anne Bogart and Tadashi Suzuki. Finding acting increasingly narrow, Haj transitioned into directing, returning to helm two productions for PlayMakers, which would serve as a prelude to his tenure to come.

The first production, in the 2004–2005 season was Stephen MacDonald's *Not About Heroes,* a taut, two-character drama about soldier-poets in the First World War. The next season closed with Haj's own adaptation of Edmond Rostand's immortal *Cyrano de Bergerac* (featuring company member Ray Dooley), a production that embraced all of the flamboyance and theatricality of its protagonist. While his later directorial work would prove to be

Left: Joseph Haj on the set of *The Importance of Being Earnest*, 2009–2010. Set Design by Marion Williams. Courtesy of PRC.

Below: McKay Coble. Photograph by John Masters Photography. Courtesy of McKay Coble.

Right: *The Illusion*, 2006–2007. Jeffrey Blair Cornell as Matamore. Costume Design by Marion Williams, Set Design by McKay Coble, Lighting Design by Justin Townsend. Costume for Matamore made by Amanda Phillips. Photograph by Jon Gardiner. Courtesy of PRC.

The Little Prince, 2007–2008. Costume Design by McKay Coble for Leslie Shires as the Little Prince and Heaven Chijerae Stephens, Joy Jones, and Flor De Liz Perez as the Wall of Roses; 2008–2009 for Derrick Ledbetter as the Little Prince and Marianne Miller, Joy Jones, and Flor De Liz Perez as the Wall of Roses. Wall of Roses made by Rachel E. Pollock. Courtesy of McKay Coble.

The Little Prince, 2007–2008 and 2008–2009. Kenneth P. Strong as The Aviator. Costume and Set Design by McKay Coble, Lighting Design by Justin Townsend. Photograph by Jon Gardiner. Courtesy of PRC.

stylistically varied, Haj would blend the rigor of the first production with the expressivity of the latter in all of his subsequent projects.

From his first season in 2006, Joseph Haj led a renaissance in the company's development by expanding its audiences, extending the mission, and rebranding PlayMakers for a meaningful place in the resident theatre landscape of the 21st century.

Key changes included:

(1) Committing to artistic diversity and increased access for audiences.
(2) Establishing a Second Stage season in the Elizabeth Price Kenan Theatre.
(3) Strengthening ties between PlayMakers and the local, Triangle, and Triad communities.

Haj's dedication to these goals transformed the company in a variety of ways, resulting in upgrades to the physical building itself, impacting play selection and season planning, widening the range of invited guest artists, and making the graduate actors of the M.F.A. program a more integral part of the company through frequent casting.

Seasons expanded as the Kenan Theatre became a shared venue between the professional and undergraduate companies, enriching the latter through example and resources. Launched in 2006 as PRC² to complement the main-stage productions continuing on the Paul Green stage, the PRC² productions further diversified the PlayMakers experience, targeting exciting and innovative material for shorter runs, and allowing each of those projects to find their audience—whether from subscribers or newcomers.

Pride and Prejudice, 2008–2009. Graduate students Flor De Liz Perez as Kitty Bennet and Allison Altman as Lydia Bennet. Costume Design by Camille Assaf, Set Design by Junghyun Georgia Lee, Lighting Design by Marcus Doshi. Costumes made by Judy Adamson (Kitty Bennett) and Amy Page (Lydia Bennett); hats made by Rachel E. Pollock. Photograph by Jon Gardiner. Courtesy of PRC.

PRC logo, used from 2009 to 2015.
Courtesy of PRC.

The initial productions of the new venture, Doug Wright's tour de force *I Am My Own Wife*, directed by Julie Fishell, and the hip-hop spoken word poetry piece *Universes*, set down markers for the range of offerings to come. Haj himself solo-performed Raja Shehadeh's *When the Bulbul Stopped Singing*. It was followed by Mike Wiley's *Witness to an Execution*; performance artist Taylor Mac's *The Young Ladies Of . . .*; Samuel Beckett's *Happy Days* with Julie Fishell and Ray Dooley; Joan Didion's *The Year of Magical Thinking*; Ray Dooley performing Lisa Peterson and Denis O'Hare's one-man *An Iliad;* Loudon Wainwright III's musical drama *Surviving Twin;* and the world premiere of Mike Daisey's monologue drama, *The Story of the Gun.*

Alongside these efforts, Joseph Haj cast an eye toward the future, fostering deeper engagement in schools and off-campus venues, enlarging the program of student matinees, and initiating an off-season training opportunity for middle and high school students by inaugurating the Summer Youth Conservatory.

Beginning in 2007–2008, company members and guest artists mentored energetic participants in classes and workshops in all facets of theatre, allowing the SYC students to explore their creativity while gaining a practical understanding of craft and the professional discipline of the stage. The new initiative culminated in an annual performance featuring Summer Youth Conservatory participation at every level of production. With their high degree of attention and accomplishment, those productions have turned what began as an experiment into a Triangle institution. Conservatory offerings to date have ranged from *The Music Man, A Midsummer Night's Dream, Sweeney Todd: The Demon Barber of Fleet Street, Hairspray, Bye Bye Birdie,* and *Bright Star.*

Through nine exciting seasons, Joseph Haj led the company with empathy, joy, and consummate artistry. His probing insights and quiet authority marked such radically different and thrilling productions as Tony Kushner's adaptation of Pierre Corneille's meditation on love, *The Illusion*; David Edgar's

The Life and Adventures of Nicholas Nickleby, 2009–2010. *Left to right*: Flor De Liz Perez (partially obscured), Kahlil Gonzalez-Garcia, John Brummer, and Derrick Ledbetter as Milliners, Lenore Field as Miss Knag, and Sarah Berk as a Milliner. Costume Design by Jan Chambers, Set Design by McKay Coble, Lighting Design by Tyler Micoleau. Costume for Miss Knag made by Lisa Raymond; bonnets made by Rachel E. Pollock. Photograph by Jon Gardiner. Courtesy of PRC.

Left: The Life and Adventures of Nicholas Nickleby, 2009–2010. Costume Design by Jan Chambers for Lenore Field as Miss Knag. Courtesy of Jan Chambers.

Right: The Life and Adventures of Nicholas Nickleby, 2009–2010. Costume Design by Jan Chambers for Scott Ripley and John Brummer as Charles and Ned Cheeryble. Courtesy of Jan Chambers.

Left: *The Importance of Being Earnest*, 2009–2010. *Left to right*: Julia Coffey as Gwendolyn Fairfax and Marianne Miller as Cecily Cardew. Costume Design by Anne Kennedy, Set Design by Marion Williams, Lighting Design by Charlie Morrison. Costume for Gwendolyn Fairfax made by Samantha Cole and for Cecily Cardew made by Claire Fleming, accessories made by Rachel E. Pollock. Photograph by Jon Gardiner. Courtesy of PRC.

Right: *Fences*, 2010–2011. Inspiration collage by Jan Chambers for the set design. Courtesy of Jan Chambers.

mammoth stage incarnation of *The Life and Adventures of Nicholas Nickleby* (co-directed with recurring guest artist Tom Quaintance); and the landmark Kander and Ebb musical *Cabaret*. Equally memorable were the technically inventive, visually striking repertory set for Shakespeare's *The Tempest* and Mary Zimmerman's *Metamorphoses*. Haj shared directing duties with Dominique Serrand, several energetic cast members, and a reflecting pool awash with fifteen tons of water on the Paul Green Theatre stage.

That repertory pairing was another major development initiated by Haj, who had long had the dream of reviving a rotating model by coupling productions within the established PlayMakers framework of individual runs. The first experiment was in the 2007–2008 season with tandem productions of two Pulitzer Prize winners, *Doubt* by John Patrick Shanley, and Suzan-Lori Parks' *Topdog/Underdog*. 2008–2009 saw the pairing of Tennessee Williams's memory play *The Glass Menagerie*, with Lisa Kron's autobiographical *Well*, the latter directed by Haj. The creative and technical lessons learned in preparing

Angels in America,
2010–2011. The Angels
are blessing Matthew
Carlson as Prior Walker.
The Angels (and all
other roles) were per-
formed by Christian
Conn, Jeffrey Blair
Cornell, Julie Fishell,
Avery Glymph, Kathryn
Hunter-Williams, Jeffrey
Meanza, and Marianne
Miller. Costume and
Makeup Design by Jan
Chambers, Set Design
by Narelle Sissons,
Lighting Design by
Pat Collins. Costumes
made by Judy Adamson
from digitally printed
fabrics. Photograph by
Jon Gardiner. Courtesy
of PRC.

these repertory sets allowed works of epic length and scale to make their company debuts. Three back-to-back seasons saw *Nicholas Nickleby* in 2009–2010,
featuring twenty-five actors and a record 150 costumes; both parts of Tony
Kushner's instant classic *Angels in America* in their entirety in 2010–2011; and
in 2011–2012 *The Making of a King*, joining Shakespeare's *Henry IV, Parts I
and II* and *Henry V*, which were co-directed by Haj and Mike Donahue.
Lorraine Hansberry's classic *A Raisin in the Sun* was contrasted with Bruce
Norris' scorching follow-up *Clybourne Park* in 2012–2013, while Haj raised the
creative stakes even further by directing both the aforementioned *The Tempest*
and *Metamorphoses* simultaneously in 2013–2014. Rounding out the repertory
series in 2014–2015 were Shakespeare's *A Midsummer Night's Dream* joined
by Haj's production of Stephen Sondheim and James Lapine's evergreen *Into
the Woods*.

Other notable Joseph Haj productions include:

- 2007–2008: Peter Shaffer's *Amadeus* starred Ray Dooley as a consummate Antonio Salieri. Haj reconceived the production three years later for
  performance with the North Carolina Symphony, with Dooley reprising
  his role.
- 2008–2009: The lesser seen Shakespeare *Pericles, Prince of Tyre* inventively
  combined Eastern and Western dramatic conventions, and was later re-
  mounted and acclaimed elsewhere.

Cabaret, 2012–2013. Nathaniel Claridad as Bobby, Taylor Mac as the Emcee, Katie Paxton as Lulu. Costume Design by Jennifer Caprio, Set Design by Marion Williams, Lighting Design by Josh Epstein. Photograph by Jon Gardiner. Courtesy of PRC.

Amadeus, 2007–2008. Ray Dooley as Antonio Salieri. Costume Design by Bill Black, Set Design by McKay Coble, Lighting Design by Marcus Doshi. Costume for Salieri made by Daniel Weger. Photograph by Jon Gardiner. Courtesy of PRC.

- 2010–2011: Haj's first musical, Roger Miller and William Hauptman's *Big River: The Adventures of Huckleberry Finn*, captured the spirit of Mark Twain while rising to the challenge of staging fluid scenes along the banks and suggesting the vast waters of the Mississippi River itself. Musical accompaniment was by the Red Clay Ramblers, who had appeared in the show's pre-Broadway run at San Diego's La Jolla Playhouse in 1985.

Red, 2012–2013. Matt Garner as Ken and Stephen Caffrey as Rothko. Costume Design by McKay Coble, Set Design by Jan Chambers, Lighting Design by Charlie Morrison. Photograph by Jon Gardiner. Courtesy of PRC.

Haj also welcomed new voices and visions during his tenure, garnering Play-Makers a higher-profile as well as important grants and awards.

- Directors Tom Quaintance, Raelle Myrick-Hodges, Brendon Fox, Mike Donahue, Vivienne Benesch, Libby Appel, and Desdemona Chiang, would all lead multiple productions for the company, with Benesch hired as the next Producing Artistic Director.
- Associate Artistic Director Jeffrey Meanza, like Haj a graduate of UNC-Chapel Hill's Professional Actors Training Program, left his own mark on the PlayMakers legacy through a number of memorable onstage performances and the collaborative ethic he fostered as an administrator.
- In 2010, PlayMakers was awarded the first of a pair of grants from the Andrew W. Mellon Foundation, which were used to support summer residencies for six prestigious national theatre companies over as many years, including Pig Iron Theatre Company, SITI Company, The TEAM, Rude Mechanicals, Critical Mass, and Elevator Repair Service.
- Significant artistic and faculty hires included scenic and costume designer Jan Chambers, lighting designer Kathy Perkins, and company actress Julia

Gibson. Each of these theatre artists making indelible contributions during Haj's years with the company.

- Managerial support throughout these seasons came from Rob Franklin Fox, Heidi Reklis, Hannah Grannemann, and Michele Weathers.
- Color-conscious casting and progressive programming informed both the mainstage and second stage seasons, while productions such as Tanya Barfield's *Blue Door*; Heather Raffo's *9 Parts of Desire*; Sonja Linden's *I Have Before Me a Wonderful Document Given to Me by a Young Lady from Rwanda*; August Wilson's *Fences*; Nilaja Sun's *No Child*; Katori Hall's *The Mountaintop*; and Roger Guenveur Smith's *Rodney King* gave issues of race and representation provocatively dramatic form.
- In 2013, PlayMakers was awarded an inaugural Leaders in Diversity Award by the Triangle Business Journal, in recognition of Joseph Haj's furthering of the company's mission during his tenure. Haj's fine body of work is exemplified in the titles above, and especially in the world premiere of Mike Wiley's Freedom Riders drama, *The Parchman Hour*, at the start of the 2011–2012 season.

Joseph Haj spoke of his eclectic sweep in 2015, telling an interviewer: "I love Shakespeare, I love a Lisa Kron play, I love a great musical, I love work of traditional theater makers and I love devised work, work we don't understand," concluding, "How we champion artists on the edge is important." That last

point is central to Haj's aesthetic, revisiting the key theme of a galvanizing symposium address presented by Haj to his professional peers a year earlier:

> "Our edges roll in towards the center, and we make a terrific mistake if we are not nurturing those artists and companies who make work in ways that we don't immediately understand, or at first blush even know how to fully appreciate. And so I encourage you to make the work you most need to make. Choose people who are unlike you. Choose people who work in paradigms other than your own. Choose generosity. Choose love. Make room. There is truly such abundance."

During his time with PlayMakers, Joseph Haj led by example, wholeheartedly investing in each of these principles. Their cumulative effect on the company remains enormous.

As further proof of his faith in opportunity, in 2015 Joseph Haj became the eighth Artistic Director of the Guthrie Theater, the nation's most prestigious regional theatre organization. His appointment exemplifies—and fulfills—all that he worked so tirelessly and creatively to achieve while in Chapel Hill.

GREGORY KABLE has been a production dramaturg on nearly 50 PRC productions since 1997. He has covered the alphabet in two dozen directing projects ranging from Alan Ayckbourn through Tennessee Williams, and Georg Buchner to Lanford Wilson, including works by Strindberg, Sam Shepard, and Sondheim.

RESOLUTELY ENGAGING THE FUTURE |

VIVIENNE BENESCH

By Cecelia Moore

 In early 2016, Vivienne Benesch assumed her new role as Producing Artistic Director of PlayMakers Repertory Company. She came from Chautauqua Theater Company, where she had served as artistic director for ten seasons. A graduate of Brown University (BA) and the Tisch School of the Arts at New York University (MFA), Benesch also had extensive acting and teaching experience.

She was familiar with UNC-Chapel Hill because she had directed at PRC, including Sara Ruhl's *In The Next Room* (2011), *Red* by John Logan (2012), and *Love Alone* by Deborah Salem Smith (2014). Her first production in her new role was Chekhov's *Three Sisters* in January 2016.

Benesch sensed the opportunity that the University and the local community provides for artists interested both in teaching and in developing new ideas for the theatre. "There is room here to be creative and take risks and connect with people, an intellectual and cultural community pushing you to do great work," she observed in an interview shortly after her appointment. One of her goals was to develop work that engaged more communities with PRC.

As she noted in an early blogpost: "The face of America is changing. I am humbled with the charge of serving this great company in a time that I believe will see great transformation in the American Theater—no longer holding up a mirror to just a narrow view of nature—but to the expansive reality of what the human race actually looks like and experiences today. And we're lucky, because PlayMakers is the perfect home for such a collision of art and change to take hold."

In Fall 2017, Benesch and PRC's plans received an emphatic affirmation from long-time PlayMakers supporter Joan H. Gillings. She committed to a $12 million gift for PlayMakers and the Department of Dramatic Art, the

Vivienne Benesch.
Photograph by Alison
Sheehy. Courtesy of
PRC.

Three Sisters, 2015–2016. Front row (*left to right*): Samuel Byron Frazelle as Vladimir Karlovich Roday and Jorge Donoso as Aleksei Petrovich Fedotik (*backs to camera*). Second row (*left to right*): Allison Altman as Irena Sergeyevna (on the floor). Third row: Schuyler Scott Mastain as Vasilii Vasilyevich Solyony, Ray Dooley (partially obscured) as Ivan Romanovich Chebutykin, Benjamin Curns as Andrei Sergeyevich Prozorov, Carey Cox as Natalya Ivanova, Julie Fishell as Anfisa (partially obscured), Joshua David Robinson as Aleksander Ignatyevich Vershinin, Marinda Anderson as Olga Sergeyevna, Ariel Yoder as Maria (Masha) Sergeyevna (almost completely obscured), Daniel Pearce as Fyodor Iliyich Kulygin. Behind the ladder (*left to right*): Emma Gutt and Katy Castaldi as members of the ensemble. On the platform above: Cellist Isabel Castellvi. Costume Design by Tracy Christensen, Set Design by Alexis Distler, Lighting Design by Peter West. Costumes made by Emily Plonski (Irena), Max Epps (Olga), Erin Abbenante (Natalya), Katie Keener (Masha). Photograph by Jon Gardiner. Courtesy of PRC.

We Are Proud to Present, 2015–2016. Preparations in the rehearsal room. Front row (*left to right*): Caroline Strange as Black Woman, Carey Cox as Sarah, Schuyler Scott Mastain as White Man, and Nathaniel Kent as Another White Man. Second row: Myles Bullock as Black Man. Set and Costume Design by Junghyun Georgia Lee, Lighting Design by Porsche McGovern. Photograph by Rosalie Preston. Courtesy of PRC.

largest single donation to the performing arts in the University's history. This endowment supports more funding for students in the MFA acting, costume production, and technical production programs; education and outreach programs, including a new "Mobile Shakespeare" initiative; an artist-in-residency program; and new play development. The newly-named Joan H. Gillings Center for Dramatic Art recognizes this transformative gift.

Benesch's first four PRC seasons have demonstrated creativity and a commitment to engage with pressing questions of the moment. Productions have nodded to the one hundred-plus years of theatre history at UNC, reinterpreted the classics, and sought out new regional material relevant to the community's future. In October 2016, PRC staged Arthur Miller's *The Crucible*, which had been part of its first season as a professional repertory company 40 years earlier. The new production, however, placed the action in the round and used modern elements to relate the work to questions about community and citizenship in the midst of a national election that year. In similar ways, Benesch's productions of other classics had a new relevancy for audiences. The 2017–2018 season included the ever-popular Lerner and Loewe musical *My Fair Lady*, based on George Bernard Shaw's play *Pygmalion*. PRC's production contrasted the popular songs with an emphasis on the original play's gender and class tensions, which remain surprisingly relevant today. That same season, PRC paired the Moliere classic *Tartuffe* in repertory with a newer work, *The Christians* by Lucas Hnath, to consider the role of religion in peoples'

The Cake, 2017–2018. Julia Gibson as Della. Costume Design by Junghyun Georgia Lee, Set Design by Jan Chambers, Lighting Design by Burke Brown. Cake fabricated by Properties Master Andrea Bullock. Stage painting by Scenic Charge Artist Jessica Secrest. Photograph by HuthPhoto, Courtesy of PRC.

Intimate Apparel, 2016–2017. *Left to right*: Rasool Jahan as Esther and Shanelle Nicole Leonard as Mayme. Costume Design by Bobbi Owen, Set Design by Junghyun Georgia Lee, Lighting Design by Xavier Pierce. Costume for Esther made by Judy Adamson and for Mayme made by Max Epps. Photograph by Jon Gardiner. Courtesy of PRC.

lives. The character of Tartuffe is the prototypical hypocrite who hides his ambitions behind traditional religious piety. PRC's production employed a multi-racial cast to encourage the audience to consider how race, gender and sexuality influence religious experience.

Two new plays in the 2017–2018 season showed how local and regional material could be applicable to the national moment. *The Cake* by Bekah

Sense and Sensibility, 2017–2018. Ray Dooley as Mrs. Jennings. Costume Design by Olivera Gajic, Set Design by Peter Ksander, Lighting Design by Cecilia Durbin. Costume made by Erin Torkelson. Photograph by HuthPhoto, Courtesy of PRC.

Brunstetter and *Leaving Eden* by Mike Wiley (with music and lyrics by Laurelyn Dossett) featured North Carolina-based playwrights who are also UNC-Chapel Hill alumni. Both works drew from local subject matter—gay marriage and conservative Christians in *The Cake*; race, identity, and change in a small town in *Leaving Eden*—while vividly portraying divisions present in much of the United States.

In September, PRC opened its 2019–2020 season with a new stage adaptation of Richard Wright's novel *Native Son*. Some forty years earlier, an adaptation by UNC alumnus Paul Green was the first production in the new theatre building named in his honor. The choice was a nod to the past and a call to envision a brighter future. In her *Playbill* message, Benesch wrote about the new season's theme of past and present:

"With the fruits of our many legacies surfacing around us in sometimes beautiful and sometimes harrowing ways, it's a peculiar and important time to be grappling with our Legacy/NOW." It was to be a season of new journeys, of confronting tradition and self-discovery. A young writer returned to her past on a family farm in the comedy *Dairyland* by Heidi

Tartuffe, 2017–2018. *Left to right*: Ray Dooley as Orgon, Shanelle Nicole Leonard as Dorine, Brandon Haynes as Damis, Kathryn Hunter-Williams as Madame Pernelle, April Mae Davis as Mariane. Costume Design by Anne Kennedy, Set Design by Alexis Distler, Lighting Design by Oliver Watson. Costume for Orgon made by Michelle Bentley, for Madame Pernelle made by Robin Ankerich, and for Mariane made by Danielle Soldat. Photograph by HuthPhoto. Courtesy of PRC.

Tartuffe, 2017–2018. Kelly Ann Johns, Wardrobe Supervisor for PRC and Wig Master for *Tartuffe*, completing preparations backstage for dress rehearsal. Photograph by Donn Young. Courtesy of PRC.

Armbruster; while Branden Jacobs-Jenkins re-envisioned the 15th century morality play *Everyman* about life's ultimate journey in *Everybody*. The musical *Ragtime* (based on the novel by E. L. Doctorow) depicted the complex story of turn of the 20th century America, challenging audiences to face the racism and violence often present in the nation's history.

In PlayMakers' first production of *Julius Caesar*, Shakespeare's play about power, politics, and the uncertain nature of human affairs, a diverse cast brought a fresh, modern perspective. The show opened in early March 2020, only to be cancelled early in its run, along with the remaining two productions of the season because of the COVID-19 global pandemic. Along with the rest of the world, the theatre and department had to deal with new dangers associated with live performance and teaching.

During her tenure as Artistic Director, Vivienne Benesch and Adam Versényi, Department Chair since 2014, have worked to maintain a high level of artistic excellence while providing top quality theatrical training. They have addressed the need for more diversity and access to the arts with projects including "The Welcome Table" initiative, which works to dismantle stereotypes. They also created additional opportunities for audiences to engage more with the subject matter of productions. Marketing Director Diana Pineda and her staff including Brittany Petruzzi and Rosalie Preston have been responsible for many of these efforts.

- Important artistic and faculty hires included performers Samuel Ray Gates and Tia James (also a director and voice specialist), voice, text,

Skeleton Crew, 2018–2019. Kathryn Hunter-Williams as Faye and Samuel Ray Gates as Reggie. Costume Design by Junghyun Georgia Lee, Set Design by Jan Chambers, Lighting Design by Porsche McGovern. Stage painting by Scenic Charge Artist Jessica Secrest. Photograph by HuthPhoto. Courtesy of PRC.

and dialect specialist Gwendolyn Schwinke, and playwright Jacqueline Lawton.

- Long-time Production Manager Michael Rolleri continued to coordinate the work of support units for resident and visiting directors and for scenic, costume, lighting, and sound designers. Technical Director Adam Maxfield and Assistant Technical Director Laura Pates led the scene shop, and in 2019, Triffin Morris became Costume Director upon Judy Adamson's retirement. Morris joined an established team in the costume department that included Rachel Pollock (Crafts Artisan since 2005) and Jennifer Guadagno Bayang who was appointed Assistant Costume Director in 2014.
- Production support also came from an excellent team including Production Stage Manager Charles K. (Chuck) Bayang, who has been involved in more than eighty productions since he arrived in 2008, and Stage Manager Elizabeth Ray who joined PRC in 2013.

In her first years as artistic director at PRC, Vivienne Benesch demonstrated that she had a clear vision for what a repertory company-educational model of theatre could do. She has followed through on what she promised when she began—to take risks and to expand the range of stories on the stage. The community has responded in turn as new artists, audiences, and supporters have joined the company's ranks. What comes next will be shaped by the current moment of pause on live performances. Yet theatre has always been an

Above: Jump, 2018–2019. Assistant Technical Director Laura Pates (*left*) and Technical Director Adam Maxfield (*right*) installing rivets on the handrail for the bridge. Costume Design by Tristan Raines, Set Design by Alexis Distler, Lighting Design by Amith Chandrashaker. Photograph courtesy of Nate Pohl.

Left: Everybody, 2019–2020. David Adamson as Death. Costume and Set Design by McKay Coble. Lighting Design by Cha See. Costume made by Erin Rodgers. Photograph by HuthPhoto. Courtesy of PRC.

uncertain business, which may help explain why its practitioners are invariably resourceful, innovative, and optimistic. What is certain is that artists are essential, as Benesch noted at the start of the season, to help consider "our own part in the larger national project of reckoning, reconciliation, and renewal—as individuals, as an organization, and as a community."

CECELIA MOORE is the former University Historian for the University of North Carolina at Chapel Hill. She holds an MA in public history from North Carolina State University, and a PhD in history from UNC-Chapel Hill. She is the author of *The Federal Theatre Project in the American South: The Carolina Playmakers and the Quest for American Drama* and co-author of *UNC A to Z: What Every Tar Heel Needs to Know about the First State University*. She was the director of development for PlayMakers Repertory Company and the Department of Dramatic Art from 1995 to 1999.

AFTERWORD

By Vivienne Benesch

 I began writing this essay on August 19, 2020—the day we would have been welcoming audiences into the theatre for the first show of PlayMakers Repertory Company's 46th season. It turned out, however, that the season in front of us was going to look very different from the season that we'd planned—or from any of the seasons you've just read about in the preceding pages. The COVID-19 pandemic sweeping the nation and the world has turned gathering in public, which is at the very heart of what we do as a theater company, into something dangerous. So we, along with theater and performing arts institutions across the country, are being asked to imagine new possibilities and embrace the necessity for transformation.

"Transformation" was the theme of my inaugural season five years ago as PRC's Producing Artistic Director. It seemed a galvanizing way to usher in a new chapter for the company and, true to the word's definition (change, conversion, revolution) demonstrate my belief that theatre can have a transformational impact on individuals and profoundly contribute to building successful communities. Good stories from a multiplicity of perspectives—told well by a variety of artists invested in the craft and then shared with audiences eager to receive them—have the promise and the power to move people's hearts, change minds, and reshape worldviews.

Over the relatively short time that I've been privileged to serve the company, I have come to recognize the myriad ways in which PlayMakers has been impacting community over the last fifty years. PRC has long been recognized as a jewel of the University of North Carolina at Chapel Hill and of the region. This book chronicles this considerable achievement and rightfully celebrates the incredible accomplishments of the visionary and brave artists who created a model for one of the most unique and successful regional theaters in the nation. Indeed, in 2003 the Drama League of New York named us one of the best regional theatres in the country, and in 2014 American Theatre Magazine called PRC one of "America's leading theater companies."

I believe it is meaningful that when Arthur Housman and Tom Haas were considering a name for the professional organization in 1976, they chose to use the word *Company* in the title. We could have been PlayMakers Repertory Theatre—but we are not. The word company derives from the Latin *companio*, literally "bread fellow." We feed ourselves as a community—together—with theatre. Throughout its history, PlayMakers has fed and touched the lives of hundreds of students, thousands of artists, and now audience members.

Today, PlayMakers is one of the last professional theatres in the nation to maintain a resident company. At a moment when the industry is loudly crying out with a renewed desire and need for company—for theatrical "bread fellows"—as a best practice for making good art (and, crucially, for supporting and nurturing artists), most independent nonprofits are finding the prospect of a resident company a financial impossibility. I do not, nor should anyone, take for granted the value of UNC-Chapel Hill's commitment to maintaining ours. It is one of the major factors that will continue to distinguish PRC as one of America's leading theatre makers and educators.

One of the other features that has allowed PlayMakers to build and sustain its reputation over the years is our ability as a company to answer the call of the moment. Each artistic director has brought with them specific advances and passions that have resonated in the company and the community. The evolving representation and varied expertise of the actors, designers, staff, and faculty has influenced and shifted the nature of the work being made at any given time. Most significantly, PlayMakers position within the University— embedded in the Department of Dramatic Art—has meant that we are always surrounded by a new generation of innovators and ambitious minds that are dreaming about what's possible, unencumbered by "the way things have always been." It is and has always been our responsibility to meet these young and aspiring artists where they are, thinking forward and imagining what's next.

So in this challenging time of national and global unrest, we must plan and envision a future for PlayMakers that may not look like our past—indeed in many ways *should* not and cannot look like our past—but one that respects the past as the fertile ground and firm foundation upon which we stand to imagine a better way forward. My wish for PlayMakers in its next 50 years is that it is defined as much by its world-class craft as by its forward-thinking.

As I finish writing this essay, we still have no idea how long it will be before we can start making or sharing theatre again in the way that we have known it. The performing arts industry is one of the hardest hit by COVID-19 and will be one of the last to re-open. But, if there is a silver lining to this suspension

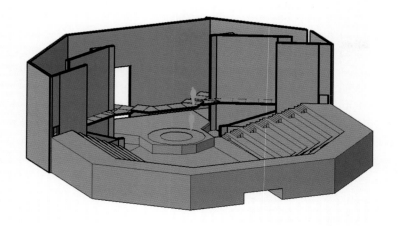

Festival Stage 3D Model, 2021. Designed by Jan Chambers and McKay Coble, 3D rendering by Kevin M. Pendergast, graduate student in Technical Production.

of public performances, it's that we are adapting and transforming perhaps more swiftly and resiliently than we thought possible. Last week, on Zoom, we workshopped the winner of the Thomas Wolfe International Play Prize, Sara Jean Accuardi's *The Storyteller*. Appropriately titled, this glistening new play provided the creative bones for a week where theatrical storytelling found a way to co-mingle with streaming technology and make something altogether new. Meanwhile, in the magnificent but all too quiet Paul Green Theatre, our graduate students in the Technical Production MFA Program, under the supervision of our skeleton production team, were building and installing not one, but two beautiful, intricate sets for productions that may well never happen in the way in which they were imagined. Such determination to keep working and keep telling stories no matter what has prompted spontaneous tears of joy and sadness in me every time I visit the Paul Green (from behind my mandatory protective armor of mask and shield).

What gives me hope is that the catharsis of gathering has proven in these last many months that it too will persist at all costs. With the absence of communal cultural events, many Americans have had the time to focus on the social justice issues of our time and come together in the streets to make their voices heard. The protests that have formed all over the country against systemic racism, police brutality, and the oppression of Black American bodies have shone a new light on the deep fissures in the foundation of our country. They have also reconfirmed the power that a group of people has to change the world with a story.

PlayMakers, along with the entire theatre industry, is in a moment of reckoning where we must chart a course to respond to these urgent stories. Not only must we continue to "hold a mirror up to nature," as Shakespeare proclaimed, but we must now risk cracking that mirror on occasion and doing better. "Transformational impact" no longer merely means the impact we have on our audiences and artists, but indeed the impact we're willing to let those audiences and artists have on us—and our own ways of operating. Are we an equitable and just theater? Are we truly doing the work that our mission statement lays out as our charge? How do we ensure that a multiplicity of perspectives does not exist only on our stages, but throughout every part of our organization? This moment of pause from "business as usual" means we have the opportunity to conduct a rigorous evaluation of our policies and practices in order to authentically embed equitable, antiracist policies into our strategic planning, our mission, our operations.

There is much that points to such transformation and growth being possible. When I joined PlayMakers in 2016, I was only the 16th female artistic director of a major professional regional theatre in the country. In the five years since I've been here in Chapel Hill that number has grown exponentially. In that time, PlayMakers has gone from being known predominantly as a home for top-notch productions of classics to also being a vibrant home for new work, having produced eight world premieres in the last four seasons. Even this year, in our virtual-only season, in addition to *The Storyteller,* we will be presenting *Edges of Time*, a world premiere by faculty and company member Jacqueline E. Lawton. And as this goes to press, we will be announcing the commissioning of two important American female writers, Bekah Brunstetter

Workshop reading in 2016–2017 for *Leaving Eden. Leaving Eden,* in the rehearsal room. Front row (*left to right*) Mike Wiley and Vivienne Benesch confer. Second row (*left to right*) Jennifer Caster and Adam Bintz (Sound Engineer).

Leaving Eden, 2017–2018. "Load in" of the set by the technical staff. First row (*left to right*): Andrea Bullock (Properties Master), Adrienne Call (Properties Artisan), and Adam Maxfield (Technical Director). Second row (*left to right*): Michael Rolleri (Production Manager), T. J. Hansen (graduate student), and Dominic Abbenante (Master Electrician). Back row: Nate Pohl (graduate student). Photograph courtesy of Jessica Secrest.

Leaving Eden, 2017–2018. The company in the opening with Tangela Large as Selah (*center*) invoking the spirits of 2016 and 1933 with the lyrics "Awake . . . Awake and heed the drum." Costume Design by McKay Coble, Set Design by Jan Chambers, Lighting Design by Mary Louise Geiger. Selah's costume made by Danielle Soldat. Stage painting by Scenic Charge Artist Jessica Secrest. Photograph by HuthPhoto. Courtesy of PRC.

and Charly Evon Simpson (who are both familiar to PlayMakers audiences) to write new works specifically for our company. Inclusive representation in both our acting company and in our cadre of guest artists has radically increased over the last several years, and we have also consistently seen gender parity in our season programming. The 2018–19 season boasted a lineup of all women directors on the mainstage—something that is still next to unheard of in major theatres in America. We have also taken a page from our own Carolina Playmakers history and started going back "on the road" with a touring program called PlayMakers Mobile. In our twenty-first century edition, however, we now send a streamlined production to a variety of community centers, Title I schools, public libraries, and rehabilitation centers and perform entirely free of charge.

This may sound like I'm patting myself and PlayMakers on the back—and that is far from the case. Because what challenges me and energizes me is how far we still have to go. The country just elected its first African-American and Asian-American woman as vice-president. Who will be the first woman of color to serve PlayMakers as Artistic Director or Managing Director? Transformation was indeed the theme of my inaugural season, but what I have come to learn is that that act of dynamic change and evolution, in the theatre we produce as well as in the company that produces it, is the life force that will keep PlayMakers relevant and vital for what I hope is another hundred years. I wish I had a Magic 8–Ball to see into that future.

But in the meantime, here at what Carolina great Charles Kuralt called "the University of the People" I am engaged with a community (broadly speaking several communities) that make me proud to be among them and with whom I am inspired—whether it be on stage, back stage, in the shops and offices, in the class or rehearsal rooms—to serve in the trenches.

VIVIENNE BENESCH, Producing Artistic Director for PlayMakers Repertory Company, has had a wide-ranging career as a director, producer, educator, and performer. In 2018, she directed the world premiere of Noah Haidle's *Birthday Candles* for Detroit Public Theatre and will direct it again starring Debra Messing on Broadway—once the COVID-19 pandemic ends.

Appendix I

PlayMakers Repertory Company Productions, 1975–1976 to Present

SEASON 1975–1976

PlayMakers Repertory Company

The Mad Dog Blues by Sam Shepard; Directed by Tom Haas.

Isadora Duncan Sleeps with the Russian Navy by Jeff Wanshel; Directed by Tom Haas. (World Premiere).

Holiday by Philip Barry; Directed by Joseph Coleman.

Hot Grog by Jim Wann and Bland Simpson (Book and Lyrics); Directed by Tom Haas. (Co-production with Peg Leg Productions).

Johnny Johnson by Paul Green with Music by Kurt Weill; Directed by Tom Haas and Joseph Coleman.

That's the Spirit by Joe Simmons and Mike Dixon; Directed by Tom Haas and Joseph Coleman (Matinee series for public schools in Spring 1976).

SEASON 1976–1977

PlayMakers Repertory Company

Poe and the House of Usher by Tom Haas and Joseph Coleman; Directed by Joseph Coleman. (Toured public schools in Western North Carolina in Fall 1976 and was the matinee series for public schools in Spring 1977).

The Crucible by Arthur Miller; Directed by Arthur Housman.

All's Well That Ends Well by William Shakespeare; Directed by Tom Haas.

A History of the American Film by Christopher Durang; Directed by Bill Ludel.

Once in a Lifetime by George S. Kaufman and Moss Hart; Directed by Tom Haas.

SEASON 1977–1978

PlayMakers Repertory Company

A Streetcar Named Desire by Tennessee Williams; Directed by Bill Ludel.

Equus by Peter Shaffer; Directed by Tom Haas.

Play It Again, Sam by Woody Allen; Directed by Bill Peters.

Hamlet by William Shakespeare; Directed by Tom Haas.

Uncommon Women and Others by Wendy Wasserstein; Directed by Mary Gallagher.

Ah, Wilderness! by Eugene O'Neill; Directed by Tom Haas.

Mister Roberts by Thomas Heggen and Joshua Logan; Directed by Tom Rezzuto.

SEASON 1978–1979

PlayMakers Repertory Company

Dracula, The Vampire King by Tom Haas; Directed by Tom Haas.
Threads by Jonathan Bolt; Directed by Jonathan Bolt.
Cold Storage by Ronald Ribman; Directed by Errol Selsby.
Long Day's Journey into Night by Eugene O'Neill; Directed by Tom Haas.
Macbeth by William Shakespeare; Directed by Tom Haas.
You Can't Take It With You by George S. Kaufman and Moss Hart; Directed by
    Bill Peters.

SEASON 1979–1980

PlayMakers Repertory Company

Of Mice and Men by John Steinbeck; Directed by Arthur Housman.
Sherman the Peacemaker by James Reston, Jr.; Directed by Tom Haas.
Side by Side by Sondheim by Stephen Sondheim (Music and Lyrics) and Ned Sherrin
    (Continuity); Directed by Errol Selsby.
The Gin Game by Donald L. Coburn; Directed by Amy Saltz.
Othello by William Shakespeare; Directed by Tom Haas.
No Time for Comedy by S.N. Behrman; Directed by Tom Haas.

SEASON 1980–1981

PlayMakers Repertory Company

The Cocktail Party by T.S. Eliot; Directed by Harold Scott.
Mrs. Warren's Profession by George Bernard Shaw; Directed by David Rotenberg.
Ghosts by Henrik Ibsen, Translated by Kai Jurgensen and Robert Schenkkan;
    Directed by Tunc Yalman.
Agnes of God by John Pielmeier; Directed by David Rotenberg.
The Fourposter by Jan de Hartog; Directed by Peter Bennett.
A Midsummer Night's Dream by William Shakespeare; Directed by
    Stephen Willems.

SEASON 1981–1982

PlayMakers Repertory Company

The Front Page by Ben Hecht and Charles MacArthur; Directed by
    David Rotenberg.
Betrayal by Harold Pinter; Directed by David Rotenberg.
The Glass Menagerie by Tennessee Williams; Directed by Gregory Boyd.
Angel Street by Patrick Hamilton; Directed by Gregory Boyd.
Mobile Hymn by Robert Litz; Directed by David Rotenberg. (World Premiere).
Twelfth Night by William Shakespeare; Directed by David Rotenberg.

PlayMakers Repertory Company

Life on the Mississippi by Mark Twain, Adapted by Bland Simpson and
   Tommy Thompson; Directed by David Rotenberg.
A Moon for the Misbegotten by Eugene O'Neill; Directed by Gregory Boyd.
The Greeks: Part 1 The Cursed and Part II The Blessed by Euripides and Homer,
   Adapted by John Barton and Kenneth Cavander from the Original Translation
   by Kenneth Cavander; Directed by Gregory Boyd and David Rotenberg.
Pygmalion by George Bernard Shaw; Directed by Gregory Boyd.

PlayMakers Repertory Company

As You Like It by William Shakespeare; Directed by Gregory Boyd.
The Hostage by Brendan Behan; Directed by Robert W. Tolan.
The Importance of Being Earnest by Oscar Wilde; Directed by Douglas Johnson.
   (One of three plays in "PlayFest '84).
Travesties by Tom Stoppard; Directed by Gregory Boyd. (One of three plays in
   "PlayFest '84).
Dracula: A Musical Nightmare by Douglas Johnson (Book and Lyrics) and
   John Aschenbrenner (Music); Directed by Douglas Johnson. (One of three plays
   in "PlayFest '84).

PlayMakers Repertory Company

Three Guys Naked from the Waist Down by Jerry Colker (Book and Lyrics) and
   Michael Rupert (Music); Directed by Andrew Cadiff. (World Premiere).
The Last Song of John Proffit by Tommy Thompson; Directed by David Rotenberg.
   (One-person show featuring Tommy Thompson).
Ring Round the Moon by Jean Anouilh; Directed by Douglas Johnson.
Our Town by Thornton Wilder; Directed by Gregory Boyd.
Measure for Measure by William Shakespeare; Directed by Gregory Boyd.
   (One of three plays in "PlayFest '85").
Curse of the Starving Class by Sam Shepard; Directed by Gregory Boyd. (One of
   three plays in "PlayFest '85").
Cloud 9 by Caryl Churchill; Directed by Ben Cameron. (One of three plays in
   "PlayFest '85").
Cyrano de Bergerac by Edmond Rostand, Translated by Brian Hooker; Directed
   by Gregory Boyd and Nels Hennum.

PlayMakers Repertory Company

She Stoops to Conquer by Oliver Goldsmith; Directed by Douglas Johnson.

The Storm by Alexander Ostrovsky, Adapted by David Hammond; Directed by David Hammond.

The Dining Room by A.R. Gurney, Jr.; Directed by Ben Cameron. (One of three plays in "PlayFest '86: An American Celebration").

The Guiteau Burlesque by Dick Beebe; Directed by Evan Yionoulis. (One of three plays in "PlayFest '86: An American Celebration," World Premiere).

Clarence Darrow: A One-Man Play by David W. Rintels; Directed by Jack Fletcher. (One of three plays in "PlayFest '86: An American Celebration;" One-person show featuring James Pritchett).

Much Ado About Nothing by William Shakespeare; Directed by David Hammond.

SEASON 1986–1987

PlayMakers Repertory Company

Look Homeward, Angel by Ketti Frings, Based on the novel by Thomas Wolfe; Directed by David Hammond.

Waiting for Godot by Samuel Beckett; Directed by David Hammond.

The Matchmaker by Thornton Wilder; Directed by Evan Yionoulis.

A Doll's House by Henrik Ibsen; Directed by Christian Angermann. (One of three plays in "PlayFest '87: Three Plays about Women").

The Human Voice by Jean Cocteau; Directed by Arthur Housman. (One of three plays in "PlayFest '87: Three Plays about Women;" One-person show featuring Cigdem Onat).

LuAnn Hampton Laverty Oberlander by Preston Jones; Directed by Craig Turner. (One of three plays in "PlayFest '87: Three Plays about Women").

A Midsummer Night's Dream by William Shakespeare; Directed by David Hammond.

SEASON 1987–1988

PlayMakers Repertory Company

Romeo and Juliet by William Shakespeare; Directed by David Hammond.

Orphans by Lyle Kessler; Directed by Maureen Heffernan.

Affectionately Yours, Fanny Kemble by Eugenia Rawls; Directed by Eugenia Rawls. (One-person show featuring Eugenia Rawls).

A Child's Christmas in Wales by Dylan Thomas, Adapted by Jeremy Brooks and Adrian Mitchell; Directed by Christian Angermann.

Mourning Becomes Electra by Eugene O'Neill; Directed by David Hammond.

On The Verge (or The Geography of Yearning) by Eric Overmyer; Directed by Christian Angermann.

The Beggar's Opera by John Gay, Adapted by David Hammond; Directed by David Hammond.

PlayMakers Repertory Company

The Marriage of Figaro by Pierre Augustin Caron de Beaumarchais, Adapted by
Peter Jeffries; Directed by David Hammond.
The Road to Mecca by Athol Fugard; Directed by Christian Angermann.
A Child's Christmas in Wales by Dylan Thomas; Directed by Christian Angermann.
For Lease or Sale by Elizabeth Spencer; Directed by David Hammond.
Misalliance by George Bernard Shaw; Directed by Maureen Heffernan.
The Taming of the Shrew by William Shakespeare; Directed by David Hammond.

SEASON 1989–1990

PlayMakers Repertory Company

The Cherry Orchard by Anton Chekhov; Directed by David Hammond.
Old Times by Harold Pinter; Directed by Kathryn Long.
The Nutcracker: A Play by E.T.A. Hoffman, Adapted by Karl Joos; Directed by
David Hammond.
Love's Labour's Lost by William Shakespeare; Directed by Charles Newell.
True West by Sam Shepard; Directed by Martin L. Platt.
The Rivals by Richard Brinsley Sheridan; Directed by David Hammond.

SEASON 1990–1991

PlayMakers Repertory Company

You Never Can Tell by George Bernard Shaw; Directed by David Hammond.
Nothing Sacred by George F. Walker; Directed by Eugene Lesser.
The Nutcracker: A Play by E.T.A. Hoffman, Adapted by David Hammond;
Directed by David Hammond.
The Miser by Molière, Translated by Sara O'Connor; Directed by
William Woodman.
Scenes from American Life by A. R. Gurney, Jr.; Directed by Bill Gile.
Pericles by William Shakespeare; Directed by David Hammond.

SEASON 1991–1992

PlayMakers Repertory Company

Hard Times by Charles Dickens, Adapted by Stephen Jeffreys; Directed by
David Hammond.
A Shayna Maidel by Barbara Lebow; Directed by Ray Dooley.
The Nutcracker: A Play by E.T.A. Hoffman, Adapted by David Hammond;
Directed by David Hammond.
Who's Afraid of Virginia Woolf? by Edward Albee; Directed by William Woodman.
Eleemosynary by Lee Blessing; Directed by Kathryn Long.
Twelfth Night by William Shakespeare; Directed by Martin L. Platt.

PlayMakers Repertory Company

The Little Foxes by Lillian Hellman; Directed by Stephen Stout.
Prelude to a Kiss by Craig Lucas; Directed by Ray Dooley.
The Nutcracker: A Play by E.T.A. Hoffman, Adapted by David Hammond;
    Directed by DeDe Corvinus.
Tartuffe by Molière, Translated by Sara O'Connor; Directed by David Hammond.
Some Americans Abroad by Richard Nelson; Directed by Evan Yionoulis.
Hamlet by William Shakespeare; Directed by David Hammond.

SEASON 1993–1994

PlayMakers Repertory Company

The Grapes of Wrath by John Steinbeck, Adapted by Frank Galati; Directed by
    David Hammond.
Marvin's Room by Scott McPherson; Directed by Ray Dooley.
Beauty and the Beast by Tom Huey; Directed by Michael Wilson.
Death of a Salesman by Arthur Miller; Directed by Jeffrey Hayden.
Arms and the Man by George Bernard Shaw; Directed by David Hammond.
Love Letters by A.R. Gurney, Jr.; Directed by Jeffrey Hayden. (Special UNC-
    Chapel Hill bicentennial performance featuring Eva Marie Saint and
    George Grizzard).
The Winter's Tale by William Shakespeare; Directed by Charles Newell.

SEASON 1994–1995

PlayMakers Repertory Company

A Streetcar Named Desire by Tennessee Williams; Directed by Michael Wilson.
2 by Romulus Linney; Directed by David Hammond.
Beauty and the Beast by Tom Huey; Directed by Michael Wilson.
The Visit by Friedrich Dürrenmatt, Translated by Maurice Valency; Directed by
    David Hammond.
Charley's Aunt by Brandon Thomas; Directed by Daniel Fish.
Macbeth by William Shakespeare; Directed by David Wheeler.

SEASON 1995–1996

PlayMakers Repertory Company

Othello by William Shakespeare; Directed by David Hammond.
A Perfect Ganesh by Terrence McNally; Directed by Daniel Fish.
Beauty and the Beast by Tom Huey; Directed by Christopher Baker.
The Seagull by Anton Chekhov, Translated by Paul Schmidt; Directed by
    Michael Wilson.
The Two-Character Play by Tennessee Williams; Directed by Michael Wilson.
    (Special benefit performance featuring Keir Dullea and Elizabeth Ashley).

From the Mississippi Delta by Endesha Ida Mae Holland; Directed by
  Tazewell Thompson.

Arcadia by Tom Stoppard; Directed by David Hammond.

SEASON 1996–1997

PlayMakers Repertory Company

Cymbeline by William Shakespeare; Directed by Tazewell Thompson.

Three Tall Women by Edward Albee; Directed by John Rando.

The Nutcracker: A Play by E.T.A. Hoffman, Adapted by David Hammond;
  Directed by David Hammond.

The Death of Papa by Horton Foote; Directed by Michael Wilson.

Molly Sweeney by Brian Friel; Directed by Susie Fuller.

A Little Night Music by Stephen Sondheim (Music and Lyrics) and Hugh Wheeler
  (Book); Directed by David Hammond.

SEASON 1997–1998

PlayMakers Repertory Company

As You Like It by William Shakespeare; Directed by Tazewell Thompson.

Skylight by David Hare; Directed by John Rando.

The Nutcracker: A Play by E.T.A. Hoffman, Adapted by David Hammond;
  Directed by Adam Versényi.

Master Class by Terrence McNally; Directed by Tazewell Thompson.

Mrs. Klein by Nicholas Wright; Directed by Andre Ernotte.

The Threepenny Opera by Bertolt Brecht (Book and Lyrics) and Kurt Weill (Music),
  Translated by Robert David MacDonald; Directed by Bartlett Sher.

SEASON 1998–1999

PlayMakers Repertory Company

The Tempest by William Shakespeare; Directed by Tazewell Thompson.

Gross Indecency by Moisés Kaufman; Directed by Loretta Greco.

A Christmas Carol by Charles Dickens, Adapted by William Leach; Directed by
  William Leach. (One-person show featuring Ray Dooley).

Having Our Say: The Delany Sisters' First 100 Years by Annie Elizabeth and
  Sarah "Sadie" Delany, Adapted by Emily Mann; Directed by
  Tazewell Thompson.

The Beauty Queen of Leenane by Martin McDonagh; Directed by Nagle Jackson.

Violet: A Musical by Jeanine Tesori (Music) and Brian Crawley (Libretto), Based on
  "The Ugliest Pilgrim" by Doris Betts; Directed by Drew Barr.

SEASON 1999–2000

PlayMakers Repertory Company

Constant Star by Tazewell Thompson; Directed by Tazewell Thompson.
A Delicate Balance by Edward Albee; Directed by Nagle Jackson.
An O. Henry Christmas by O. Henry with Adaptation, Music, and Lyrics by
    Peter Ekstrom; Directed by Ted Shaffner.
The Glass Menagerie by Tennessee Williams; Directed by Kent Paul.
Wit by Margaret Edson; Directed by Drew Barr.
Hay Fever by Noël Coward; Directed by Eric Woodall.

SEASON 2000–2001

PlayMakers Repertory Company

The School for Wives by Molière, Translated by Richard Wilbur; Directed by
    László Marton.
Look Homeward, Angel by Ketti Frings, Based on novel by Thomas Wolfe;
    Directed by Kent Paul.
An O. Henry Christmas by O. Henry with Adaptation, Music, and Lyrics by
    Peter Ekstrom; Directed by Ted Shaffner.
Side Man by Warren Leight; Directed by Drew Barr.
'Master Harold' and the Boys by Athol Fugard; Directed by John Dillon.
All's Well That Ends Well by William Shakespeare; Directed by David Hammond.

SEASON 2001–2002

PlayMakers Repertory Company

The Laramie Project by Moisés Kaufman and the members of Tectonic Theater
    Project; Directed by David Hammond.
The Man Who Came to Dinner by Moss Hart and George S. Kaufman; Directed
    by Michael Sexton.
Art by Yasmina Reza, Translated by Christopher Hampton; Directed by
    Ted Shaffner.
The Playboy of the Western World by John Millington Synge; Directed by
    John Dillon.
Our Town by Thornton Wilder; Directed by David Hammond.

SEASON 2002–2003

PlayMakers Repertory Company

Sunrise in My Pocket by Edwin Justus Mayer, Adapted by Jeffrey Hayden; Directed
    by Jeffrey Hayden.
Proof by David Auburn; Directed by Ted Shaffner.
Dinner with Friends by Donald Margulies; Directed by Drew Barr.
Uncle Vanya by Anton Chekhov; Directed by László Marton.
Salome by Oscar Wilde, Adapted from the original French by Matt Di Cintio;
    Directed by Trezana Beverley.

PlayMakers Repertory Company

A Prayer for Owen Meany by John Irving, Adapted by Simon Bent; Directed by David Hammond. (American Premiere).

Hobson's Choice by Harold Brighouse; Directed by Blake Robison.

King Lear by William Shakespeare; Directed by Mark Wing-Davey.

The Subject Was Roses by Frank D. Gilroy; Directed by Drew Barr.

Luminosity by Nick Stafford; Directed by David Hammond.

SEASON 2004-2005

PlayMakers Repertory Company

The Tragedy of King Richard II by William Shakespeare; Directed by David Hammond.

Not About Heroes by Stephen MacDonald; Directed by Joseph C. Haj.

Copenhagen by Michael Frayn; Directed by Drew Barr.

Yellowman by Dael Orlandersmith; Directed by Trezana Beverley.

Caesar and Cleopatra by George Bernard Shaw; Directed by David Hammond.

SEASON 2005-2006

PlayMakers Repertory Company

The Front Page by Ben Hecht and Charles MacArthur; Directed by Gene Saks.

String of Pearls by Michele Lowe; Directed by Trezana Beverley.

Frozen by Bryony Lavery; Directed by Drew Barr.

God's Man in Texas by David Rambo; Directed by Anthony Powell.

Cyrano de Bergerac by Edmond Rostand; Directed by Joseph C. Haj.

SEASON 2006-2007

PlayMakers Repertory Company

The Underpants by Carl Sternheim, Adapted by Steve Martin; Directed by Gene Saks.

Tuesdays with Morrie by Jeffrey Hatcher and Mitch Albom; Directed by Joan Darling.

Stones in His Pockets by Marie Jones; Directed by John Feltch.

The Bluest Eye by Toni Morrison, Adapted by Lydia R. Diamond; Directed by Trezana Beverley.

The Illusion by Pierre Corneille, Adapted by Tony Kushner; Directed by Joseph C. Haj.

PRC in the Kenan

I Am My Own Wife by Doug Wright; Directed by Julie Fishell. (One-person show featuring John Feltch).

Universes by Mildred Ruiz-Sapp and Steven Sapp; Directed by Steven Sapp.

Summer Youth Conservatory

Oliver! by Lionel Bart (Music and Lyrics), Based on *Oliver Twist* by Charles Dickens; Directed by Tom Quaintance.

PlayMakers Repertory Company

Romeo and Juliet by William Shakespeare; Directed by Davis McCallum.

Crimes of the Heart by Beth Henley; Directed by John Feltch.

The Little Prince by Antoine de Saint-Exupéry, Adapted by Rick Cummins and John Scoullar; Directed by Tom Quaintance.

Topdog/Underdog by Suzan-Lori Parks; Directed by Raelle Myrick-Hodges.

Doubt by John Patrick Shanley; Directed by Drew Barr.

Amadeus by Peter Shaffer; Directed by Joseph C. Haj.

PRC²

When the Bulbul Stopped Singing by Raja Shehadeh, Adapted by David Grieg; Directed by Ellen Hemphill. (One-person show featuring Joseph Haj).

2.5 Minute Ride by Lisa Kron; Directed by Mark Brokaw. (A one-person show featuring Lisa Kron).

Witness to an Execution by Mike Wiley; Directed by Kathryn Hunter-Williams. (One-person show featuring Mike Wiley).

Summer Youth Conservatory

The Music Man by Meredith Willson (Book, Music, and Lyrics); Directed by Tom Quaintance.

SEASON 2008–2009

PlayMakers Repertory Company

Pericles, Prince of Tyre by William Shakespeare; Directed by Joseph C. Haj.

Blue Door by Tanya Barfield (Book and Lyrics) and Larry Gilliard, Jr. (Music); Directed by Trezana Beverley.

The Little Prince by Antoine de Saint-Exupéry, Adapted by Rick Cummins and John Scoullar; Directed by Tom Quaintance.

The Glass Menagerie by Tennessee Williams; Directed by Libby Appel. (In rotating repertory with *Well*).

Well by Lisa Kron; Directed by Joseph C. Haj. (In rotating repertory with *The Glass Menagerie*).

Pride and Prejudice by Jane Austen, Adapted by Jon Jory; Directed by Timothy Douglas.

PRC²

In The Continuum by Danai Gurira and Nikkole Salter; Directed by Liesl Tommy.

The Young Ladies Of . . . by Taylor Mac; Directed by Tracy Trevett. (One-person show featuring Taylor Mac).

9 Parts of Desire by Heather Raffo; Directed by Emily Ranii. (One-person show featuring Elizabeth Huffman).

Summer Youth Conservatory

A Midsummer Night's Dream by William Shakespeare; Directed by
　　Tom Quaintance.

PlayMakers Repertory Company

Opus by Michael Hollinger; Directed by Brendon Fox.
The Life and Adventures of Nicholas Nickleby by Charles Dickens, Adapted by
　　David Edgar; Directed by Joseph C. Haj and Tom Quaintance.
All My Sons by Arthur Miller; Directed by Davis McCallum.
The Importance of Being Earnest by Oscar Wilde; Directed by Matthew Arbour.

PRC²

The Last Cargo Cult by Mike Daisey; Directed by Jean-Michele Gregory. (One-
　　person show featuring Mike Daisey).
The Big Bang by Mildred Ruiz-Sapp, Steven Sapp, Gamal Chasten, and
　　William Ruiz (aka Ninja); Directed by UNIVERSES.
*I Have Before Me a Remarkable Document Given to Me by a Young Lady From
　　Rwanda* by Sonja Linden; Directed by Raelle Myrick-Hodges.

Summer Youth Conservatory

Drood by Rupert Holmes, Based on *The Mystery of Edwin Drood* by
　　Charles Dickens; Directed by Tom Quaintance.

PlayMakers Repertory Company

As You Like It by William Shakespeare; Directed by Joseph C. Haj.
Fences by August Wilson; Directed by Seret Scott.
Shipwrecked! An Entertainment by Donald Margulies; Directed by
　　Tom Quaintance.
Amadeus: PlayMakers at the NC Symphony; Directed by Joseph C. Haj. (Based
　　on the play by Peter Shaffer).
Angels in America by Tony Kushner; Directed by Brendon Fox.
Big River by Roger Miller (Music and Lyrics) and William Hauptman (Book);
　　Directed by Joseph C. Haj.

PRC²

Happy Days by Samuel Beckett; Directed by Rob Melrose.
Exit Cuckoo (Nanny in Motherland) by Lisa Ramirez; Directed by Colman
　　Domingo. (One-person show featuring Lisa Ramirez).
The Year of Magical Thinking by Joan Didion; Directed by Mark DeChiazza.
　　(One-person show featuring Ellen McLaughlin).

PlayMakers Repertory Company

In the Next Room (or The Vibrator Play) by Sarah Ruhl; Directed by Vivienne Benesch.

The Parchman Hour by Mike Wiley; Directed by Mike Wiley. (World Premiere).

Who's Afraid of Virginia Woolf? by Edward Albee; Directed by Wendy C. Goldberg.

The Making of a King: Henry IV & V by William Shakespeare; Directed by Joseph C. Haj and Mike Donahue.

Noises Off by Michael Frayn; Directed by Michael Michetti.

PRC²

A Number by Caryl Churchill; Directed by Mike Donahue.

No Child by Nilaja Sun; Directed by Hal Brooks. (One-person show featuring Nilaja Sun).

Penelope by Ellen McLaughlin and Sarah Kirkland Snider (Music); Directed by Lisa Rothe. (One-person show featuring Ellen McLaughlin).

Summer Youth Conservatory

Urinetown: The Musical by Mark Hollmann (Music and Lyrics) and Greg Kotis (Book and Lyrics); Directed by Julie Fishell and Jeff Stanley.

SEASON 2012–2013

PlayMakers Repertory Company

Red by John Logan; Directed by Vivienne Benesch.

Imaginary Invalid by Molière, Adapted by David Ball; Directed by Dominique Serrand. (World Premiere of the Adaptation).

It's a Wonderful Life: A Live Radio Play by Joe Landry (Adaptation); Directed by Nelson T. Eusebio, III.

A Raisin in the Sun by Lorraine Hansberry; Directed by Raelle Myrick-Hodges. (In rotating repertory with *Clybourne Park*).

Clybourne Park by Bruce Norris; Directed by Tracy Young. (In rotating repertory with *A Raisin in the Sun*).

Cabaret by Joe Masteroff (Book), John Kander (Music), and Fred Ebb (Lyrics); Directed by Joseph C. Haj.

PRC²

An Iliad by Lisa Peterson and Denis O'Hare; Directed by Jesse Berger. (One-person show featuring Ray Dooley).

And God Created Great Whales by Rinde Eckert (Created, Written, and Composed); Directed by David Schweizer.

Spring Training by Mildred Ruiz-Sapp, Steven Sapp, Gamal Chasten, and William Ruiz (aka Ninja); Directed by Chay Yew. (World Premiere).

Summer Youth Conservatory

Sweeney Todd: The Demon Barber of Fleet Street by Stephen Sondheim and
   Hugh Wheeler; Directed by Tom Quaintance.

SEASON 2013–2014

PlayMakers Repertory Company

The Mountaintop by Katori Hall; Directed by Raelle Myrick-Hodges.
Metamorphoses by Mary Zimmerman; Directed by Joseph C. Haj and
   Dominique Serrand. (In rotating repertory with *The Tempest*).
The Tempest by William Shakespeare; Directed by Joseph C. Haj. (In rotating
   repertory with *Metamorphoses*).
Private Lives by Noël Coward; Directed by Sean Daniels.
Love Alone by Deborah Salem Smith; Directed by Vivienne Benesch.
Assassins by Stephen Sondheim (Music and Lyrics) and John Weidman (Book);
   Directed by Mike Donahue.

PRC²

Surviving Twin by Loudon Wainwright III; Directed by Joseph C. Haj. (One-
   person show featuring Loudon Wainwright III).
The Story of the Gun by Mike Daisey; Directed by Jean-Michele Gregory. (One-
   person show featuring Mike Daisey; World Premiere).
Hold These Truths by Jeanne Sakata; Directed by Jeanne Sakata. (One-person show
   featuring Joel de la Fuente).

Summer Youth Conservatory

Hairspray by Mark O'Donnell and Thomas Meehan (Book), Marc Shaiman (Music
   and Lyrics), and Scott Wittman (Lyrics); Directed by Desdemona Chiang.

SEASON 2014–2015

PlayMakers Repertory Company

Vanya and Sonia and Masha and Spike by Christopher Durang; Directed by
   Libby Appel.
A Midsummer Night's Dream by William Shakespeare; Directed by Shana Cooper.
   (In rotating repertory with *Into the Woods*).
Into the Woods by Stephen Sondheim (Music and Lyrics) and James Lapine (Book);
   Directed by Joseph C. Haj. (In rotating repertory with *A Midsummer Night's
   Dream*).
Trouble in Mind by Alice Childress; Directed by Jade King Carroll.
An Enemy of the People by Henrik Ibsen, Adapted by Arthur Miller; Directed by
   Tom Quaintance.
4000 Miles by Amy Herzog; Directed by Desdemona Chiang.

PRC²

Rodney King by Roger Guenveur Smith; Directed by Roger Guenveur Smith.
   (One-person show featuring Roger Guenveur Smith).
Wrestling Jerusalem by Aaron Davidman; Directed by Michael John Garcés.
   (One-person show featuring Aaron Davidman).
Mary's Wedding by Stephen Massicotte; Directed by Cody Nickell.

Summer Youth Conservatory

Guys and Dolls by Frank Loesser (Music and Lyrics) and Jo Swerling and Abe Burrows
   (Book), Based on short stories by Damon Runyon; Directed by Jeffrey Meanza.

SEASON 2015–2016

PlayMakers Repertory Company

Disgraced by Ayad Akhtar; Directed by Shishir Kurup.
Seminar by Theresa Rebeck; Directed by Michael Dove.
Peter and the Starcatcher by Rick Elice (Play) and Wayne Barker (Music); Directed
   by Brendon Fox.
Three Sisters by Anton Chekhov, New Version Adapted by Libby Appel; Directed
   by Vivienne Benesch.
We Are Proud to Present by Jackie Sibblies Drury; Directed by Desdemona Chiang.
Sweeney Todd: The Demon Barber of Fleet Street by Stephen Sondheim (Music and
   Lyrics); Hugh Wheeler (Book); Directed by Jen Wineman.

PRC²

Uncle Ho to Uncle Sam by Trieu Tran with Robert Egan; Directed by Robert Egan.
   (One-person show featuring Trieu Tran).
Highway 47 by K.J. Sanchez; Directed by Lisa Portes. (One-person show featuring
   K.J. Sanchez).
The Real Americans by Dan Hoyle; Directed by Charlie Varon. (One-person show
   featuring Dan Hoyle).

Summer Youth Conservatory

Violet: A Musical by Jeanine Tesori (Music) and Brian Crawley (Libretto), Based on
   "The Ugliest Pilgrim" by Doris Betts; Directed by Matthew Steffens.

SEASON 2016–2017

PlayMakers Repertory Company

Detroit '67 by Dominique Morisseau; Directed by Lisa Rothe.
The Crucible by Arthur Miller; Directed by Desdemona Chiang.
The May Queen by Molly Smith Metzler; Directed by Vivienne Benesch. (Regional
   Premiere)
Intimate Apparel by Lynn Nottage; Directed by Raelle Myrick-Hodges.

Twelfth Night by William Shakespeare; Directed by Jerry Ruiz.

My Fair Lady by Alan Jay Lerner (Book and Lyrics) and Frederick Loewe (Music); Directed by Tyne Rafaeli.

PRC²

Draw the Circle by Mashuq Mushtaq Deen; Directed by Chay Yew. (World Premiere).

De Profundis by Oscar Wilde, Adapted by Brian Mertes and Jim Findlay; Directed by Brian Mertes. (One-person show featuring Nicole Villamil).

Mr. Joy by Daniel Beaty; Directed by Vivienne Benesch. (One-person show featuring Tangela Large).

Summer Youth Conservatory

Bye Bye Birdie by Michael Stewart (Book), Charles Strouse (Music), and Lee Adams (Lyrics); Directed by Michael Perlman.

SEASON 2017–2018

PlayMakers Repertory Company

The Cake by Bekah Brunstetter; Directed by Jeffrey Meanza.

Sense and Sensibility by Kate Hamill, Based on the novel by Jane Austen; Directed by Taibi Magar.

Dot by Colman Domingo; Directed by Nicole A. Watson.

Tartuffe by Molière, Adapted by David Ball; Directed by Saheem Ali. (In rotating repertory with *The Christians*).

The Christians by Lucas Hnath; Directed by Preston Lane. (In rotating repertory with *Tartuffe*).

Leaving Eden by Mike Wiley with Laurelyn Dossett (Music and Lyrics); Directed by Vivienne Benesch. (World Premiere).

PRC²

Count by Lynden Harris; Directed by Kathryn Hunter-Williams. (World Premiere co-produced with the Hidden Voices Collective).

A Christmas Carol by Charles Dickens, Adapted by William Leach; Directed by Michael Perlman. (One-person show featuring Ray Dooley).

"A" Train by Anne Torsiglieri; Directed by Risa Brainin. (One-person show featuring Anne Torsiglieri).

Summer Youth Conservatory

Cabaret by Joe Masteroff (Book), Jon Kander (Music), and Fred Ebb (Lyrics); Directed by Tracy Bersley.

PlayMakers Repertory Company

Sherwood: The Adventures of Robin Hood by Ken Ludwig; Directed by Jessie Austrian.

Skeleton Crew by Dominique Morisseau; Directed by Valerie Curtis-Newton.

She Loves Me by Joe Masteroff (Book), Jerry Bock (Music), and Sheldon Harnick (Lyrics); Directed by Kirsten Sanderson.

Jump by Charly Evon Simpson; Directed by Whitney White.

Life of Galileo by Bertolt Brecht; translated into English by John Willett; Directed by Vivienne Benesch.

How I Learned to Drive by Paula Vogel; Directed by Lee Sunday Evans.

PRC²

Temples of Lung and Air by Kane Smego; Directed by Joseph Megel. (StreetSigns Center for Literature and Performance's one person show featuring Kane Smego; World premiere).

Bewilderness by Zachary Fine; Directed by Zachary Fine. (World premiere).

Your Healing is Killing Me by Virginia Grise and Florinda Bryant; Directed by Shayok Misha Chowdhury. (One-person show featuring Florinda Bryant).

Summer Youth Conservatory

Bright Star by Steve Martin (Music, Book, Story) and Edie Brickell (Music, Lyrics, Story); Directed by Tracy Bersley.

SEASON 2019–2020

PlayMakers Repertory Company

Native Son by Nambi E. Kelley, Based on the novel by Richard Wright; Directed by Colette Robert.

Dairyland by Heidi Armbruster; Directed by Vivienne Benesch.

Ragtime by Stephen Flaherty (Music), Lynn Ahrens (Music), and Terrence McNally (Book); Directed by Zi Alikhan.

Everybody by Branden Jacobs-Jenkins; Directed by Orlando Pabotoy.

Julius Caesar by William Shakespeare; Directed by Andrew Borba.

PRC²

No Fear and Blues Long Gone: Nina Simone by Howard L. Craft; Directed by Kathryn Hunter-Williams. (One-person show featuring Yolanda Rabun; World Premiere).

The Amish Project by Jessica Dickey; Directed by Sarah Elizabeth Wansley. (One-person show featuring Kathryn Metzger).

PlayMakers Repertory Company

Temples of Lung and Air by Kane Smego; Directed by Joseph Megel. (StreetSigns Center for Literature and Performance's one person show featuring Kane Smego; An encore performance).

The Storyteller: A Virtually Staged Reading by Sara Jean Accuardi; Directed by Vivienne Benesch.

A Christmas Carol by Charles Dickens, Adapted by William Leach; Directed by Michael Perlman. (One person audio drama featuring Ray Dooley).

Love, Loss and What I Wore by Nora Ephron and Delia Ephron; Based on the book by Ilene Beckerman. Directed by Vivienne Benesch. (Special benefit performance featuring Marin Hinkle, Camryn Manheim, and Debra Messing, and PRC company members Julia Gibson, Kathryn Hunter-Williams, and Tia James and PRC Fellow Sarita Ocón).

Blood Done Sign My Name by Timothy B. Tyson; Adapted by Mike Wiley; Directed by Mike Wiley. (One-person show featuring Mike Wiley).

As You Like It by William Shakespeare; Directed by Tia James.

Edges of Time by Jacqueline E. Lawton; Directed by Jules Odendahl-James. (One-person show featuring Kathryn Hunter-Williams; World Premiere).

Appendix II

Department of Dramatic Art Faculty, 1975–1976 to Present

University drama departments are careful to hire faculty members who can succeed both in the classroom and as part of theatrical activities. The presence of a regional theatre housed within an academic department on a college campus means that even more careful attention must be paid to ensure their success in the classroom and on (or back) stage. The 136 individuals listed below have all had permanent appointments in the Department of Dramatic Art (part-time or full time) between the 1975–1976 academic year (when PlayMakers Repertory Company (PRC) began) and the date of this publication. They have all had classroom responsibilities—some of them have won teaching awards—and the vast majority of them have been actively engaged with the professional company. Others, including guest artists, have also been involved in the classroom in a variety of ways: offering workshops and guest lectures, teaching for part of a semester, or co-teaching a course. Many graduate students also taught while completing their MFA degrees.

Dominic Abbenante (b. 1983)

Lecturer, lighting/media/projection designer, and master electrician for PlayMakers Repertory Company. Teacher of lighting design and modern Irish drama. Degrees from Indiana State University (BS) and San Diego State University (MFA). Appointed as Master Electrician in 2013 and began teaching in 2016, both of which he continued until 2019, when he left to become Technical Events Manager for the Kenan-Flagler Business School at UNC-Chapel Hill.

Pamela S. Absten (b. 1967)

Visiting Assistant Professor and vocal coach for PRC. Teacher of voice and speech. Degrees from West Virginia State College (BA) and California Institute of the Arts (MFA). Active during the 1996–1997 season and the corresponding academic year.

David A. Adamson (b. 1944)

Lecturer and PlayMakers Repertory Company member who made his first appearance in *Equus* in the 1977–1978 season. Teacher of acting, directing, and theatre literature. Degrees from the University of Northern Iowa (BA) and UNC-Chapel Hill (MFA, LDA); Vietnam War veteran (US Army). On the faculty from 1995 until his retirement in 2020.

Judy (Judith L.) Adamson (b. 1945)

Professor of the Practice, Costume Director for PRC, and head of the MFA program in Costume Production. Teacher of costume production including draping, couture methods, and period pattern after spending fourteen years at Barbara Matera, Ltd., the premiere New York City costume house. Degree from the University of Northern Iowa (BA). 2012 recipient of the Distinguished Achievement Award in Education from USITT for advocacy for costume technicians and the distinction of the costume production program at UNC-Chapel Hill. On the faculty from 1993 until her retirement as Professor Emerita in 2019.

Hope Alexander-Willis (b. 1947) (aka Hope Alexander)

Visiting Artist who taught in the Department of Dramatic Art and performed with PRC—including *Moon for the Misbegotten* and *As You Like It*—after appearing for several years with the Berkeley Rep (where she worked with Greg Boyd who brought her to UNC-Chapel Hill). Teacher of acting and directing. On the faculty from 1982 to 1984 and leader of numerous workshops since then, in between acting on stage, on television, and in motion pictures, including *The Princess Diaries I* and *The Princess Diaries II*.

Christian Angermann (b. 1950)

Visiting Assistant Professor and director for PlayMakers Repertory Company. Teacher of directing. Degrees from Yale University (BA) and the Yale University School of Drama (MFA). On faculty from 1986–1989 when he left to pursue directing opportunities at theatres including the Minetta Lane Theatre and the Provincetown Players.

Daniel Banks (b. 1965)

Teaching Associate Professor and director of staged readings for PRC. Teacher of acting with a specialization in Hip-Hop, he is Co-Director of DNAWORKS, an organization that fosters "Dialogue and Healing through the Arts." Degrees from Harvard University (BA) and the Tisch School of the Arts at New York University (MA, PhD). He directed both *We the Griot* (a devised performance workshop) as part of Dramatic Art's "Welcome Table Initiative," and *Dreaming Emmett* (a staged reading). On the faculty in the Spring 2018 Semester.

Patricia (Pat) R. Barnett (1927–1999)

Associate Professor of Dramatic Art and performer with PlayMakers Repertory Company. Teacher of stage speech and acting. Degrees from St. Catherine College in St. Paul, MN (BA) and the University of Denver (PhD). Appointed in 1967 (after appearing on stage and touring with the USO), she became the first woman to direct for the Carolina Playmakers when *The Chinese Chalk Circle* opened in December 1967. Retired as Associate Professor Emerita in 1995.

Christopher R. Baker (b. 1963)

Visiting Assistant Professor and dramaturg for PRC. Teacher of theatre history and literature. Degrees from Northwestern University (BS) and the Theater Institute for Advanced Theatre Training at Harvard University (MFA). On the faculty from 1995 to 1998, when he left to become literary manager at Hartford Stage.

Milly S. Barranger (b. 1937)

Alumni Distinguished Professor, Chair of the Department of Dramatic Art, and Executive Producer of PlayMakers Repertory Company, 1982–1999. Teacher of theatre history and literature. Degrees from the University of Montevallo (formerly Alabama College, Montevallo) (BA) and Tulane University (MA, PhD). Dean Emerita of the College of Fellows of the American Theatre, and a prolific author and skilled administrator, she was appointed in 1982 and retired as Alumni Distinguished Professor Emerita in 2001.

Glenna Batson (b. 1948)

Carroll A. Kyser Guest Lecturer and Teacher of the Alexander Technique for graduate students in the Professional Actor Training Program (PATP). Degrees from University of Wisconsin at Madison (BA), Columbia University (MA), and the Rocky Mountain University of Health Professions (ScD). On the faculty from 2004 to 2007, when she joined the Department of Physical Therapy at Winston-Salem State University, where she retired as professor emerita in 2012.

Saura Bartner (1947–2003)

Carroll A. Kyser Guest Lecturer and Teacher of the Alexander Technique for graduate students in the Professional Actor Training Program (PATP). Degrees from Rutgers University (BA) and Columbia University (MA). On the UNC-Chapel Hill faculty from 1996 until her untimely death in 2003.

Pete (Peter) Baselici (b. 1949)

Assistant Professor and technical director and lighting designer with PRC. Teacher of technical methods and lighting design. Degrees from Elon University (BA) and Florida State University (MFA). On the faculty from 1975 until 1978, when he left to develop and market lighting control systems. Baselici retired as Senior Product Manager at Hubbell Control Solutions in Austin, Texas.

Jennifer Guadagno Bayang (b. 1971)

Teaching Assistant Professor and Assistant Costume Director for PRC. Teacher of costume management and flat-pattern. Degrees from Nazareth College (BA) and Boston University (MFA). She came to UNC-Chapel Hill in 2014 after working for four years as a draper at Syracuse Stage.

Dick Beebe (1954–2008)

Lecturer and playwright-in-residence 1986–1987. The cast for the world premiere of his play, *The Guiteau Burlesque*, during the PRC 1985–1986 season included Joseph Haj, at the time a graduate student in the department. Teacher of playwriting. Degrees from Emerson College (BA) and Yale University School of Drama (MFA).

Vivienne Benesch (b. 1967)

Professor of the Practice and Producing Artistic Director, PlayMakers Repertory Company. Degrees from Brown University (BA) and New York University's Tisch School of the Arts (MFA). Teacher of performance practice. Recipient of the 2017 Zelda Fichandler Award and a 2015 OBIE Award. Appointed in 2016 after directing and performing in a variety of venues and serving as Artistic Director at Chautauqua Theater Company from 2004 to 2016.

Tracy Bersley (b. 1973)

Assistant Professor and movement coach for PlayMakers Repertory Company. Teacher of movement. Degrees from California Lutheran University (BA) and Syracuse University (MFA). A director as well as a choreographer she is a founding member of the Red Bull Theatre Company in New York. She joined the faculty in 2017.

Jade R. Bettin (b. 1979) (aka Jade Papa)

Adjunct Assistant Professor, and costume designer and costume maker for PRC. Teacher of costume history. Degrees from the University of Northern Iowa (BA) and UNC-Chapel Hill (MFA). On the faculty from 2006 to 2016, when she became Curator of the Textile and Costume Collection in The Design Center at Thomas Jefferson University.

Karen C. Blansfield (b. 1951)

Adjunct Assistant Professor and dramaturg for PRC. Teacher of theatre literature and history. Degrees from East Carolina University (BA, MA) and UNC-Chapel Hill (PhD). A scholar of modern theatre including playwright Michael Frayn, she was on the faculty from 1999 to 2005.

Greg Boyd (b. 1951)

Associate Professor, Artistic Director for PlayMakers Repertory Company, and head of the Professional Theatre Training Program now known as the Professional Actor Training Program (PATP). Teacher of acting and directing. Degrees from the University of California, Berkeley (BA) and Carnegie Mellon University (MFA). Mr. Boyd was on the faculty from 1981 to 1985, when he left to become artistic director at StageWest in Springfield, Massachusetts. Four years later, he became artistic director of the Alley Theatre in Houston, Texas.

Laurie A. Boyd (b. 1951) (aka Laurie Gayle Boyd)

Assistant Professor and resident choreographer and performer for PRC. Teacher of movement. Degrees from University of California, Berkeley (BA) and Connecticut College (MFA). She was on the faculty from 1982 to 1984.

Minda Brooks (b. 1971)

Visiting Lecturer and dramaturg for PRC. Teacher of theatre history and literature. Degrees from UNC-Chapel Hill (BA) and the University of Colorado at Boulder (MA). On the faculty from 1998 to 2000, when she left to become the Director of the Benjamin N. Duke Scholarship Program at Duke University.

Bess Brown (1958–2005) (aka Mary Elizabeth Brown; Bess Brown Kregal)

Visiting Assistant Professor and performer with PRC. Teacher of acting. Degrees from Buffalo State College (BA) and the American Conservatory Theater (MFA). She was on the faculty in the 1988–1989 academic year when she appeared as Elsa in *The Road to Mecca*. Ms. Brown left Chapel Hill in 1989 to return to her native Buffalo, where she was a much-honored actress on local stages until her untimely death in 2005.

Ben Cameron (b. 1954)

Visiting Assistant Professor and Literary Manager for PlayMakers Repertory Company from 1984 to 1986. Teacher of theatre history and literature. Degrees from UNC-Chapel Hill (BA) and the Yale University School of Drama (MFA). After leaving Chapel Hill, he held senior-level administrative positions in a number of arts organizations, including the National Endowment for the Arts, the Doris Duke Charitable Foundation, and Theatre Communications Group.

Janet A. (Jan) Chambers (b. 1954)

Professor and Resident Scenic and Costume Designer for PlayMakers Repertory Company. Teacher of scene design, make-up, and costume design. Degrees from University of Tennessee (BFA) and the University of Illinois (MFA). Resident set and costume designer for Archipelago Theatre and a member of the faculty in the Department of Theatre Studies at Duke University from 1999 to 2006, she came to UNC-Chapel Hill in 2007.

McKay Coble (b. 1957)

Professor, Resident Scenic and Costume Designer for PlayMakers Repertory Company, and Chair of the Department of Dramatic Art from 2005 to 2013. She also served as the Chair of the Faculty at Carolina from 2009–2011. Teacher of design and decorative arts. Degrees from UNC-Chapel Hill (BA, MFA). Joined the faculty in 1986 after serving as production manager and head shopper for Barbara Matera Ltd. in New York City.

Carla Coleman (b. 1973) (aka Carla Coleman Prichard)

Lecturer. Teacher of play analysis and theatre history and literature. Degrees from UNC-Chapel Hill (MA, PhD). On faculty from 2004 to 2006, when she left to join the faculty at the University of South Carolina.

Michael Connolly (b.1951) (aka Kieran Connolly)

Visiting Assistant Professor and resident actor for PlayMakers Repertory Company. Teacher of acting. Degrees from the College of the Holy Cross (AB), Illinois State University (MA), and Indiana University (PhD). He served on the faculty from 1983 to 1985, when he accepted a faculty appointment at Southern Methodist University.

Jeffrey Blair Cornell (b.1960)

Teaching Professor, Associate Chair, and PRC company member. Mr. Cornell has distinguished himself playing a wide range of characters in many PRC productions, beginning with *Othello* in the 1995–1996 season while still in graduate school. Degrees from Westminster College (BA) and UNC-Chapel Hill (MFA). Teacher of acting, voice, and theatre history and literature. He began teaching, initially on a part-time basis, in the 1998–1999 academic year and became a full time faculty member the following year.

Dorothy "DeDe" Corvinus (b. 1952)

Lecturer and performer with PRC. Teacher of acting and play analysis. Degrees from the College of Wooster (BA), the University of Washington (MFA), and the University of South Carolina (PhD). On the faculty from 1987 to 1997, when she joined the Office of Research at the UNC School of Medicine from which she retired in 2018. She has continued to perform with PRC since leaving her faculty position.

Howard Craft (b. 1970)

Piller Professor of the Practice in the Writing for the Stage and Screen program at UNC-Chapel Hill and playwright for PRC, he taught in Dramatic Art during the 2018–2019 academic year. Teacher of playwriting. Degree from North Carolina Central University (BA). Poet, essayist, and playwright, he wrote *No Fear and Blues Long Gone: Nina Simone* which opened the 2019–2020 season for PRC[2].

Jane Ann Crum (b. 1951)

Visiting Assistant Professor and dramaturg for PRC. Teacher of theatre history and literature. Degrees from Kalamazoo College (BA), the University of Texas at Austin (MFA), and the Yale University School of Drama (MFA). On the faculty from 1986 to 1988, after which she continued to teach, notably at the New School and the Yale Conservatory, and work as dramaturg. From 1997 to 2004, she served as Executive Director of The Drama League.

J. Michael Cumpsty (b. 1960)

Lecturer and member of the PRC acting company. A Morehead Scholar as an undergraduate at UNC-Chapel Hill, he earned both BA and MFA degrees at Carolina. Teacher of acting. On the faculty in the 1985–1986 academic year, Cumpsty subsequently moved to New York City, where he quickly began an especially successful career acting for film, television (*LA Law*), and theatre (including the Broadway productions of *Copenhagen* and *42nd Street*).

Robert Dagit (b. 1984)

Lecturer and Sound Designer/Engineer for PRC for more than 30 shows. Teacher of sound design and audio engineering. Degrees from the University of Southern Indiana (BA) and the University of Illinois, Urbana-Champaign (MFA). On the faculty from 2012 to 2015, he now works as a freelance sound designer/sound engineer and an adjunct faculty member.

Joan Darling (b. 1935)

Adjunct Professor and performer / director with PlayMakers Repertory Company. Teacher of acting. A highly-regarded and prolific director for television, she was one of the medium's first regular female directors, beginning with *Mary Hartman, Mary Hartman* in the mid-1970s. On the faculty from 2002 to 2008, Ms. Darling returned to semi-retired life in California with her husband, the actor and writer Bill Svanoe.

Ray Dooley (b. 1952)

Professor and resident actor for with PlayMakers Repertory Company; he also served as chair from 1999–2005 and as head of the Professional Actor Training Program from 2005 to 2018. A graduate of Hamilton College (BA) and the American Conservatory Theater (MFA), Mr. Dooley joined the faculty in 1989, initially as a guest artist. In the 2019–2020 season, PlayMakers Repertory Company celebrated "100 Plays of Ray" to commemorate his performance in 100 productions (*Ragtime* in October 2019 raised to the total to 101).

Maria Enriquez (b. 1976)

Visiting Lecturer and movement coach for PRC's production of *Peter and the Starcatcher*. Teacher of movement. Degrees from Arizona State University (MFA) and the University of Pittsburgh (PhD). She also directed *Good Girls: A Play in Five Fabulous Acts* for the PATP. She was on the faculty in the Fall 2015 Semester after which she left for a position at Pennsylvania State University-Harrisburg.

Jonathan Farwell (b. 1932)

Guest Lecturer and Artist-in-Residence with PRC. Teacher of acting. Degree from Ithaca College (BFA) as well as graduate studies at the Yale University School of Drama and with Tamara Daykarhanova of Stanislavski's Moscow Art Theatre Company. Mr. Farwell, best known for his long-running role as George Rawlins on *The Young and the Restless*, was on the faculty in the 1977–1978 academic year and appeared in *Mr. Roberts*, *Hamlet*, and *Ah, Wilderness!*

Thiago Felix da Silva (b. 1981)

Visiting Assistant Professor and movement coach for PRC. Teacher of movement, specializing in the Lucid Body technique. Degrees from the Faculdades Integradas Hélio Alonso in Rio de Janeiro (BA); studies with Fay Simpson at the Lucid Body Institute (certificate), and further training at the Michael Howard Studios. Originally from Brazil, he has taught at the Yale School of Drama and the Stella Adler Studio of Acting in New York City. On the faculty in the Spring 2019 Semester.

John Feltch (b. 1958)

Visiting Lecturer, member of the acting company, and director for PRC. Teacher of acting and introductory theater courses. Degrees from Williams College (BA) and UNC-Chapel Hill (MFA). He appeared in productions between 1983 and 1988 and again from 2003 to 2008, including Vladimir in *Waiting for Godot* and Charlotte von Mahlsdorf in *I Am My Own Wife,* one of the first PRC productions in the Kenan Theatre, which led to the formation of PRC².

Anthony Fichera (1957–2010)

Visiting Assistant Professor and Dramaturg for PlayMakers Repertory Company. Teacher of theatre literature. Degrees from California State University, Stanislaus (BA) and the Yale University School of Drama (MFA). Served on the faculty from 1992 to 1997 when he left to pursue a PhD at Florida State University. He later joined the UNC-Chapel Hill travel office and was dramaturg on additional productions from 2006 to 2010.

Zack (Zachary) Fine (b. 1978)

Visiting Lecturer and director, playwright, and performer with PlayMakers; he also wrote, directed, and performed in *Bewilderness* (a "Thoreau-ly" absurd night on Walden Pond) for PRC² in the 2018–2019 season. Teacher of acting and movement with an emphasis in clown. Degrees from Oberlin College (BA) and the University of Tennessee (MFA). He was on the faculty in the Fall 2014 Semester.

Julie Fishell (b. 1961)

Senior Lecturer and member of PRC's acting company who appeared in 54 productions. She was also one of the Founding Artists of PlayMakers Summer Youth Conservatory (SYC). Teacher of acting and directing. Degrees from the University of Evansville (BFA), The Juilliard School (Diploma), and UNC-Chapel Hill (MFA). Recipient of the Johnston Teaching Excellence Award in 2012, she was appointed in 1994. She left to join the faculty at the University of California, Santa Barbara in 2017, after making a memorable final appearance on the PRC stage as Mrs. Higgins in *My Fair Lady*.

William Fisher (b. 1956)

Visiting Lecturer and actor with PRC. Teacher of movement. Degree from the University of Indiana (BA). After studying and teaching Corporeal Mime with Etienne Decroux in Paris for four years, he was on the faculty in the 1984–1985 academic year and appeared in *Our Town*. He then moved to California, where he founded and became artistic director of the Zeta Collective (1985–1991). Afterwards he spent nineteen years on the faculty at Ohio University.

Foster Fitz-Simons (1912–1991)

Professor and performer for PlayMakers Repertory Company. Dance training and background as a member of Ted Shawn and His Men Dancers, the first all-male dance company in the United States. Degree from UNC-Chapel Hill (AB). Teacher of movement. He first taught (acting and directing) in summer 1943 and received a full-time appointment in 1945, which he held until his retirement in 1976.

Rob Franklin Fox (b. 1965)

Lecturer and General Manager of PlayMakers Repertory Company, he began his ten-year stint with PRC as assistant box office manager in 1997. Teacher of theatre management. Degrees from Belhaven College (BA) and Oklahoma City University (MBA). On the faculty from 2005 to 2007, after which he became the director of UNC-Chapel Hill's Institute for Outdoor Drama (which moved to East Carolina University during his tenure).

Peter Friedrich (b. 1964)

Visiting Lecturer. Teacher of acting and directing. Degrees from Santa Clara University (BA) and the American Conservatory Theater (MFA). A native of Chapel Hill, he spent five years teaching and directing Shakespeare in Iraq through the American University of Iraq, Sulaimani. While a member of the faculty during 2013–2014 academic year, he directed Heather Raffo's *9 Parts of Desire* for the Kenan Theatre Company (KTC), after which he joined the faculty at Millsaps College in Jackson, Mississippi.

Tina Gallegos (b. 1963) (aka Tina Brower)

Visiting lecturer and lighting designer for PRC. Teacher of lighting design. Degrees from Stephens College (BFA) and Florida State University (MFA). On the faculty in the 1993–1994 academic year, Gallegos went on to design lights for a variety of venues, among them Walt Disney Imagineering, for whom she was show lighting designer in Tokyo, Hong Kong, and Shanghai.

Ryan J. Gastelum (b. 1980)

Lecturer and Sound Designer/Sound Engineer for PlayMakers Repertory Company. Degrees from University of California, Santa Cruz (BA) and the UNC School of the Arts (MFA). Teacher of sound design and engineering. He was at Carolina from 2010 to 2012, after which he spent eight years as production manager at the Brooklyn Academy of Music. Mr. Gastelum went on to serve as production manager at the University of Washington.

Samuel Ray Gates (b. 1971)

Assistant Professor and member of the PRC acting company, appearing in *Dot* and *Leaving Eden* in his first season (2017–2018). Teacher of acting. Degrees from Hampton University (BS) and the American Conservatory Theater (MFA). After a number of years acting in regional theatres, off-Broadway, and for film and television, he joined the faculty in 2017.

Jerry Genochio (b. 1967)

Adjunct Associate Professor and Production Manager. Teacher of technical methods. Degrees from Northwest Missouri State University (BS) and Florida State University (MFA). Mr. Genochio was at UNC-Chapel Hill from 1999 to 2001, after which he spent four years as production manager at the Alabama Shakespeare Festival before becoming producing director at the Kansas City Repertory Theatre.

Julia Gibson (b. 1962)

Associate Professor, co-head of the Professional Actor Training Program, and member of the acting company for PRC, with roles including Della in *The Cake*. Teacher of acting. Degrees from The University of Iowa (BA) and New York University's Tisch School of the Arts (MFA). A playwright, director, and prolific narrator of audio books, she joined the faculty in 2013 after a successful New York-based acting career.

Jan Gist (b. 1950)

Visiting Assistant Professor and vocal coach for PRC. Teacher of voice and speech, she was a founding member of Voice and Speech Trainers Association and original editor of its national newsletter. Degrees from Carnegie Mellon University (BFA) and Wayne State University (MFA). She was at Carolina in the 1988–1989 academic year after which she joined the faculty at the University of San Diego. She has been voice, speech, and dialect coach at The Old Globe in San Diego for nearly 100 productions.

Amira Glaser (b. 1978)

Carroll A. Kyser Guest Lecturer, she teaches the Alexander Technique to students in the Professional Actor Training Program (PATP). An AmSAT certified Alexander Technique practitioner, she was trained at the American Center of the Alexander Technique in New York City and also has degrees from Sarah Lawrence College (BA), and the Pacific College of Oriental Medicine (MS). She joined the faculty in 2015.

David M. Glenn (b. 1950)

Assistant Professor and Technical Director as well as scenic and lighting designer for PlayMakers Repertory Company. Degrees from Guilford College (BA), UNC-Chapel Hill (MFA), and Howard University College of Medicine (MD). Teacher of technical production and scene design. He was on faculty from 1978 until 1982 when he became the Technical Director at Arena Stage in Washington, DC. After serving in a variety of positions at Arena Stage, Mr. Glenn became a physician specializing in emergency medicine (remaining occasionally involved with theatre).

Hannah Grannemann (b. 1979) (aka Hannah Grannemann-Isaac)

Lecturer and Managing Director for PRC from 2008 to 2014. Teacher of theatre management. Degrees from New York University's Tisch School of the Arts (BFA), the Yale University School of Drama (MFA), and the Yale University School of Management (MBA). She left PRC in 2014 to become the Executive Director of the Children's Theatre of Charlotte.

Robert F. Gross (b. 1952)

Visiting Lecturer, and dramaturg and literary manager for PlayMakers Repertory Company. Teacher of theatre history and literature. Degrees from the University of Wisconsin-Madison Madison (BA), The Ohio State University (MA), and UNC-Chapel Hill (PhD). Appointed in 1979, he left in 1981 to teach at Cornell University before joining the faculty at Hobart and William Smith Colleges in 1987, where he has had a productive career as an author, educator, and administrator.

Russell Graves (1922–2015)

Professor and performer with PlayMakers Repertory Company. Teacher of playwriting, acting, directing, and theatre history and literature. Degrees from Carnegie Institute of Technology (BFA, MFA) and Florida State University (PhD). A playwright known for his radio dramas (some of which were translated into German), he was appointed in 1951 and retired in 1992.

Tom (Thomas) Haas (1948–1991)

Associate Professor and Founding Artistic Director of PlayMakers Repertory Company. Teacher of acting and directing. Degrees from Montclair State College (BA), Cornell University (MA), and the University of Wisconsin-Madison (PhD). He was appointed in 1974 and left UNC-Chapel Hill in 1980 to become artistic director of the Indiana Repertory Theatre, where he remained until his untimely death in 1991.

Margaret Hahn (b. 1951)

Visiting Assistant Professor and administrative roles with PRC including Managing Director (1987–1989), Associate Producing Director (1986–1987), and literary manager (1983–1984). Teacher of theatre history and literature. Degrees from St. Cloud

State University (BA) and Tulane University (MFA). After leaving Chapel Hill in 1989, Ms. Hahn relocated to Washington, DC, where she worked for the National Endowment for the Arts as a theatre specialist, and later on in a variety of positions at the Edlavitch Jewish Community Center.

Joseph (Joe) Haj (b. 1964)

Professor of the Practice and Producing Artistic Director of PRC. Teacher of performance practice. Degrees from Florida International University (BFA) and UNC-Chapel Hill (MFA). Recipient of the 2014 Zelda Fichandler Award, Mr. Haj was on the faculty from 2006 to 2015, when he left to become artistic director of The Guthrie Theater.

Zachary D. (Zach) Hamm (b. 1979)

Lecturer, and Assistant Technical Director for PlayMakers Repertory Company and the Department of Dramatic Art. Teacher of technical production and methods. Degrees from Connecticut College (BA) and UNC-Chapel Hill (MFA). He left in 2007 to accept a position at Alfred University, where he currently serves as Technical Director and Clinical Associate Professor.

David Hammond (b. 1948)

Professor and Artistic Director of PRC. Teacher of acting, directing, and Shakespeare in the Theatre. Degrees from Harvard University (BA) and Carnegie Mellon University (MFA). Appointed in 1985, he spent twenty-two years at UNC, fourteen of them as artistic director. He retired as Professor Emeritus in 2006, after which he joined the faculty at Guilford College.

John Rogers Harris (b. 1962)

Assistant Professor. Teacher of theatre literature and history. Degrees from UNC-Chapel Hill (BA, MA) and The Ohio State University (PhD). He was on the faculty from 2004 to 2008, after having served a year as a Postdoctoral Fellow. He has since taught at Forsyth Technical Community College in Winston-Salem and has been a dramaturg for a variety of theatres in the Triangle area.

Justin Haslett (b. 1976)

Teaching Assistant Professor and Managing Director for PlayMakers Repertory Company. Teacher of theatre management. Degrees from Bowdoin College (BA) and the Yale University School of Drama (MFA). He was Managing Director with PRC from 2016 to 2020, after working in theatre administration for the Huntington Theatre Company and at the Merrimack Repertory Theatre.

Donna Bost Heins (b. 1964) (aka Donna Bost Prichard)

Lecturer and administrator in a variety of roles for PRC. Teacher of theatre management. Degree from the North Carolina School of the Arts (BFA). PRC General

Manager/Company Manager from 1991 to 1993, Administrative Director from 1996 to 1998, Managing Director from 2000 to 2003, and Executive Director from 2003–2006, after which she became a small business consultant and Principal with Theatre Consultants Collaborative.

Patrick Holt (b. 1967)

Lecturer, crafts artisan, and costume designer for PRC. Teacher of costume crafts. Degrees from Brigham Young University (BA) and the University of North Carolina School of the Arts (MFA). On the faculty in 2000–2001, he left to pursue additional design opportunities and to join the faculty in the School of Theatre, Film and Television at the University of Arizona. Patrick Holt is also an actor, appearing on television in *RuPaul's Drag Race* in 2009 and 2010. Since leaving Chapel Hill in 2001, he has returned occasionally to design productions for PRC.

Arthur L. Housman (1928–1990)

Professor, Chair of the Department of Dramatic Art from 1971 to 1982, and Founding Executive Director of PlayMakers Repertory Company. Teacher of theatre history and literature. Degrees from DePauw University (BA) and Iowa State University (MA, PhD). He joined the faculty in 1971 and remained active with the department and PRC until his death in 1990.

Kathryn Hunter-Williams (b. 1958)

Teaching Associate Professor and member of PRC's acting company, as well as a director for PRC, PRC², and Kenan Theatre Company (KTC) productions. Teacher of acting and theatre history and literature. Degrees from the University of North Carolina School of the Arts (BFA) and UNC-Chapel Hill (MFA). Associate Director of Hidden Voices, an arts-based non-profit organization that is dedicated to bringing life-changing stories to a wider audience, she joined the faculty in 2008.

Tom Huey (b. 1950)

Lecturer and playwright for PlayMakers Repertory Company, which produced his adaptation of *Beauty and the Beast*. Teacher of playwriting. Degrees from the University of Alabama (BA), Hollins University (MA) and UNC-Greensboro (MFA). On the faculty from 1989 to 1999, when he left to pursue writing full-time. He has also served as Playwright-in-Residence at Guilford College.

Tia James (b. 1982)

Assistant Professor, performer, director, and vocal coach for PlayMakers Repertory Company. Teacher of voice and speech, acting, and acting for the camera, with an emphasis on Miller Voice Method. Degrees from Virginia Commonwealth University (BFA) and New York University's Tisch School of the Arts (MFA). She joined the faculty in 2018 after performing on stage and television in the New York area.

Joy Javits (b. 1948)

Lecturer and movement coach/choreographer for PRC. Degree from Brown University (BA) and further study at the Yale University School of Drama. She was on the faculty from 1976, first as a short-term substitute when long-time movement teacher Foster Fitz-Simons suffered an injury, until 1982 when she began a career in private consulting. She has since founded both In the Public Eye, a communications consultancy, and the Hospital Arts Program "DooR to DooR" at UNC Hospitals.

Jeff A.R. Jones (b. 1969)

Lecturer and costume craftsperson for PRC. Teacher of costume crafts. Degrees from The College of William and Mary (BA) and Florida State University (MFA). Also a fight director and Certified Teacher of Stage Combat, he was on the faculty during the 1997–1998 academic year and PRC season, after which he left to join Carolina Ballet as Resident Designer of scenery and costumes.

Gregory Kable (b. 1958)

Teaching Professor and Dramaturg for PlayMakers Repertory Company. Popular teacher of theatre history and literature and musical theatre. Degrees from Towson University (BS), Johns Hopkins University (MFA), and the Yale University School of Drama (MFA). Since joining the faculty in 1997, he has served as dramaturg for more than fifty productions for PRC, beginning with *Mrs. Klein* and *Skylight* in his first season.

Stephanie "Stevie" Kallos (b. 1955)

Visiting Assistant Professor and PRC's Company Voice Coach. Teacher of voice and speech. Degrees from the University of Nebraska-Lincoln (BA), The Juilliard School (Diploma), and the University of Washington (MFA). She was on the faculty in the 1989–1990 academic year, after which she pursued writing full-time, leading to a successful career that includes ten novels, five short story collections, and two works of nonfiction.

Leon Katz (1919–2017)

David G. Frey Distinguished Professor and dramaturg for PlayMakers Repertory Company, after a long and distinguished career at Yale University where he retired as Professor Emeritus. Teacher of playwriting and literature. Degrees from the City College of New York (AB) and Columbia University (MA, PhD). Served on the faculty from 2004 to 2008.

Eric Ketchum (b. 1978)

Adjunct Assistant Professor and head of undergraduate production. Teacher of stagecraft, lighting design and sound design. Degrees from UNC-Chapel Hill (BA) and the University of Florida (MFA). He was on the faculty from 2007 until 2011, when he left to work as a graphic designer. In recent years, he has worked as a visual effects artist for Epic Games, a leading developer of video games.

J. Kimball King (1934–2019)

Adjunct visiting professor after retiring as Professor of English and Comparative Literature at UNC-Chapel Hill in 2004. A long-time PRC supporter, Dr. King and his wife Harriet were opening night fixtures at PRC. Teacher of theatre literature. Degrees from Johns Hopkins University (BA), Wesleyan University (MA), and the University of Wisconsin-Madison (PhD).

Nancy Lane (b. 1951)

Associate Professor and vocal coach for twenty-nine PRC productions, beginning with *You Never Can Tell* in the 1990–1991 season. Teacher of voice and speech. Degrees from the University of Iowa (BA) and the University of Minnesota (MFA). She joined the faculty in 1990, after teaching at The Juilliard School and a successful acting career in New York Ms. Lane left the faculty in 1996 to take a position in Research Triangle Park.

Jacqueline E. Lawton (b. 1978)

Associate Professor and dramaturg for PlayMakers Repertory Company. Teacher of creative dramatics, playwriting, play analysis, and theatre for social change. Degrees from the University of Texas at Austin (BS, MFA). An award-winning playwright, dramaturg, producer, and advocate for access, equity, diversity, and inclusion in the American theatre, she joined the faculty in 2015.

Todd Lawrence (b. 1974)

Lecturer and Facilities Director for PRC and the Department of Dramatic Art. Teacher of stagecraft. Degrees from Catawba College (BA) and UNC-Chapel Hill (MFA). He joined the faculty in 2009 and left in 2011 for a position at Virginia Commonwealth University, after which he returned to teach in secondary schools in the local area, including Northwood High School in Chatham County and the Durham School of the Arts.

Kenneth J. Lewis (b. 1959)

Adjunct Assistant Professor and Production Manager for PRC. Teacher of technical production and sound design. Degrees from the University of Maryland College Park (BA) and the Yale University School of Drama (MFA). A member of the faculty from 1995 to 1999, Mr. Lewis was production manager when the Center for Dramatic Art opened in 1997. He left to become production manager at Wolf Trap National Park for the Performing Arts.

Regina F. Lickteig (b. 1962) (aka Regina Neville)

Lecturer and Administrative Director for PRC from 1989 to 1991. Teacher of theatre management. Degrees from the University of Northern Iowa (BA) and the Yale University School of Drama (MFA). Before assuming the role of PRC Administrative Director in 1989, she was production stage manager during the 1988–1989 season. When she left PRC in 1991 she became Managing Director of the Marin Theatre Company in Mill Valley, California.

Ashley Lucas (b. 1979)

Assistant Professor and dramaturg for PRC. Degrees from Yale University (BA) and the University of California, San Diego (PhD). After two years at UNC-Chapel Hill as a postdoctoral fellow, she was appointed to the faculty in 2008, and subsequently taught theatre history and literature, U.S. Latino/a theatre, and theatre for social change. Dr. Lucas left at the end of the Fall 2013 Semester to accept a faculty position at the University of Michigan.

Michèl Marrano (b. 1981) (aka Michèl Marrano Holbrook)

Lecturer and resident sound designer/sound engineer for PRC. Teacher of sound design and audio engineering. Degrees from The State University of New York College at Geneseo (BA) and the University of North Carolina School of the Arts (MFA). On the faculty from 2006 to 2008, she left to take a position with Trailblazer Studios, a film production company.

Adam M. Maxfield (b. 1974)

Teaching Associate Professor and Technical Director for PlayMakers Repertory Company. Teacher of technical direction, with an emphasis on rigging, motion control, and metal fabrication. Degrees from Idaho State University (BA) and UNC-Chapel Hill (MFA). After working as a production manager in and around Las Vegas, Nevada for several years, he joined the faculty in 2010.

J. Robert (Rob) McLeod (b. 1969)

Adjunct Assistant Professor and Production Manager for PRC. Teacher of technical direction and production methods. Degrees from North Carolina State University (BA) and UNC-Chapel Hill (MFA). Active from 2006 to 2008, after which he became technical director of the Pittsburgh Public Theatre (2008–2016) before taking a similar position at Baltimore Center Stage (2016–present).

Traci Meek (b. 1973)

Lecturer and crafts artisan for PRC from 2002 to 2006. Teacher of costume crafts including dyeing and painting. Degrees from the University of Tennessee (BFA), Southern Institute of Technology (BDes), and the University of Connecticut (MFA). In 2009 she created "Meek and Wild Creations" for character and content creation (mascots and animation). She is also Screen and Visual Arts Tutor at the Southern Institute of Technology in Invercargill, New Zealand.

Jonathon A. (Jon) Mezz (1945–2002)

Assistant Professor and performer with PlayMakers Repertory Company. Teacher of theatre history and literature. Degrees from the University of Rochester (BA) and the University of Minnesota-Twin Cities (PhD). He joined the faculty in 1973 and left in 1976 to pursue acting and directing opportunities in California, where he also used his considerable talents as a classical pianist.

Michelle Moody (b. 1973)

Lecturer in the 2004–2005 academic year and Properties Director for PRC from 2003 to 2006. Teacher of period styles, scene design, and properties design. She also designed scenery for *I Am My Own Wife,* one of the first PRC productions in the Kenan Theatre, which led to the formation of PRC². Degrees from Gustavus Adolphus College (BFA) and West Virginia University (MFA). She left to become Properties Director for the Tulsa Opera. Through her business "Just a Little Moody" she is an active participant in craft and antique shows.

Triffin Morris (b. 1968)

Milly S. Barranger Professor of the Practice, Costume Director for PlayMakers Repertory Company, and head of the MFA program in Costume Production. Teacher of couture techniques and pattern-making. Degrees from the University of Wisconsin-Oshkosh (BA, BS) and the University of Wisconsin-Milwaukee (MFA). After 20 years making costumes in New York City for opera, dance, and Broadway, she joined the faculty in 2018.

David Navalinsky (b. 1971)

Associate Professor, Director of Undergraduate Production, Director of Undergraduate Studies, and lighting designer for PlayMakers Repertory Company. Teacher of production practice and first-year seminars. Degrees from Baldwin Wallace University (BA) and the University of Arizona (MFA). He joined the faculty in 2011 with a focus on undergraduate production.

Tom Neville (b. 1961)

Adjunct Associate Professor and Production Manager for PRC. Teacher of technical theatre methods. Degrees from the University of Northern Iowa (BA) and the Yale University School of Drama (MFA). On the faculty from 1987 to 1991, Mr. Neville left to become production manager at the Berkeley Repertory Theatre (1992–1996) before joining Auerbach Pollock Friedlander as a Theatre Consultant.

Karen O'Brien (b. 1965)

David G. Frey Fellow and Assistant Professor in Dramatic Art and dramaturg for PRC. Teacher of theatre history and literature, Irish drama, and directing. Degrees from The College Conservatory of Music at the University of Cincinnati (BFA, MFA) and the University of California Irvine and the University of California, San Diego (joint PhD program). On the faculty from 2009 until 2017, Dr. O'Brien left to contribute to projects involving the advancement of artistic, movement, and cultural initiatives.

Cigdem Onat (b. 1939) (aka *Çigdem* Selisik Onat, Cigdem Housman)

Lecturer and performer with PlayMakers Repertory Company. She appeared in PRC's first season as Helena in *All's Well That Ends Well*. She went on to perform other roles for PRC, including Lady Macbeth and the one-person show *The Human Voice*. Teacher of acting. Degrees from Istanbul University Faculty of Literature and UNC-Chapel Hill (MA). A leading actress of the Turkish State Theatre, she joined the faculty in 1975 and left in 1979 to teach at the University of North Carolina School of the Arts. In subsequent years she became sought after as a director and performer.

Bobbi Owen (b. 1949)

Michael R. McVaugh Distinguished Professor and Resident Costume Designer for PlayMakers Repertory Company. Teacher of costume history and theatrical design. Degrees from the University of Wisconsin-Madison (BS, MFA). Author of several books and hundreds of articles about theatrical design and designers, she joined the faculty in 1974.

John W. Parker (1909–1980)

Professor, Business Manager for the Carolina Playmakers, and secretary of the Carolina Dramatic Association. Teacher of theatre administration, literature, acting, and directing. Degrees from UNC-Chapel Hill (AB, MA). Founder of Junior Playmakers, a summer program for high school students. As a 1934 Rockefeller Fellow, he served on the staff in the drama department and then as an Instructor in the Extension Division's Bureau of Community Drama before joining the faculty in 1936. He retired as professor emeritus in 1975.

Laura Pates (b. 1989)

Teaching Assistant Professor and Assistant Technical Director for PRC and the Department of Dramatic Art. Teacher of production methods with a specialization in welding and digital imaging. Degrees from Guilford College (BA) and UNC-Chapel Hill (MFA). She joined the department in 2014.

John Patrick (b. 1979)

Associate Professor and resident vocal coach for PRC. Teacher of voice and speech, with an emphasis on the Miller Voice Method. Degrees from Texas Christian University (BFA) and Rutgers University (MFA). A co-Founder of MVM Studio, he joined the faculty in 2011. Mr. Patrick left in 2018 to provide consulting in the private sector, through JP Communication Consultants and Miller Communication Consulting.

Thomas M. Patterson (1912–1982)

Professor and Chair from 1968 to 1971. Teacher of playwriting. Degrees from the University of Texas at Austin (BA, MA). His play, *Emily* (about the poet Emily Dickinson), was produced by the Department of Dramatic Art in 1979. He joined the faculty in 1950 and retired as Professor Emeritus in 1977.

Carol Pendergrast (b. 1937)

Visiting Associate Professor and PRC's company voice coach. Degrees from San Jose State University (BA, MFA). On the faculty from 1984 to 1987, she left to freelance as a voice and speech coach as well as to perform. Ms. Pendergrast later joined the faculty at UNC-Wilmington.

Kathy A. Perkins (b. 1954)

Professor and lighting designer for PlayMakers Repertory Company. Teacher of Africa/African diaspora theatre, world drama, and lighting design. Degrees from Howard University (BFA) and the University of Michigan (MFA). On the faculty from 2012 to 2018, when she retired as Professor Emerita following a distinguished career as an author, activist, and designer. Ms. Perkins came to Chapel Hill from the University of Illinois at Urbana-Champaign where she was a member of the faculty from 1989 to 2011.

Mark Perry (b. 1970)

Teaching Assistant Professor in the Department of Dramatic Art and dramaturg for PRC. Teacher of play writing and play analysis. Degrees from the University of South Florida (BA) and the University of Iowa (MFA). His plays, *The Will of Bernard Boynton* and *A New Dress for Mona,* have been produced by the Kenan Theatre Company (KTC) for whom he has also directed. He joined the faculty in 2005.

Rick Pike (b. 1946) (aka Richard T. Pike, Jr.)

Assistant Professor and Resident Scene Designer from 1975 to 1978. Teacher of scene design. Degrees from Auburn University (BA) and Florida State University (MFA). He left Chapel Hill in 1978 to take a faculty position at Virginia Commonwealth University.

Gillian Lane Plescia (b. 1935)

Lecturer and voice consultant for PRC. Teacher of voice, dialects, and speech. Degrees from the Royal Academy of Music, London (LRAM) and Florida State University (MA). Author of several self-instructional dialect programs, she was on the faculty from 1977 to 1982.

Rachel E. Pollock (b.1972)

Teaching Assistant Professor and resident Costume Crafts Artisan and costume designer for PlayMakers Repertory Company. Teacher of costume crafts, including millinery and dyeing techniques. Degrees from the University of Tennessee (BA) and the University of New Orleans (MFA). Author of *Sticks in Petticoats* and curator of the costume crafts blog, *La Bricoleuse,* she joined the Carolina faculty in 2005.

Mary Lee Porterfield (b. 1967)

Visiting Assistant Professor and Managing Director of PRC from 1998 to 2000. Teacher of arts administration. Degrees from Wake Forest University (BA) and Brooklyn College (MFA). After several years as a performing arts administrator, Ms. Porterfield changed careers, becoming an administrator with the North Carolina Division of Child Development and Early Education, while simultaneously working on a doctoral degree at UNC-Greensboro in the Department of Human Development and Family Studies.

Craig Pratt (b. 1967)

Visiting Lecturer (1992–1993) and Assistant Technical Director for PRC. Teacher of technical direction. Degrees from Clarion University of Pennsylvania (BFA) and UNC-Chapel Hill (MFA). He left the faculty in 2003 to pursue opportunities in graphic arts and design. In 2009 he joined Todd Reed, Inc. becoming Lead Graphic Artist.

Jason T. Prichard (b.1973)

Adjunct Assistant Professor and PRC production manager (after serving as master carpenter and then assistant technical director for five years). Teacher of technical methods and production practice. Degrees from the University of Evansville (BSc) and UNC-Chapel Hill (MFA). He was production manager from 2002 to 2006, after which he became a full-time theatre consultant with Theatre Consultants Collaborative.

Alan S. Raistrick (b. 1954)

Visiting Lecturer and Technical Director. Teacher of technical direction and production methods. Degrees from Missouri Southern State College (BA) and the University of Missouri-Kansas City (MFA). On the faculty during the 1985–1986 academic year.

Bonnie N. Raphael (b. 1944)

Professor, head of the Professional Actor Training Program (1997–2005), and voice coach for PlayMakers Repertory Company. Teacher of voice, speech, and dialect. Degrees from Brooklyn College (BS), the University of Michigan (MA), and Michigan State University (PhD). On the faculty from 1997 (after being on the faculty at the University of Virginia and Harvard University) until her retirement as Professor Emerita in 2011.

Kristine Rapp (b. 1964)

Lecturer and Assistant Costume Director from 2004 to 2009. Teacher of costume shop management. Degrees from Mundelein College of Loyola University (BA) and West Virginia University (MFA). She left in 2009 to pursue opportunities as a business process manager and in 2014 became Production Workflow Manager for VStar Entertainment Group.

Tom (Tommy) Rezzuto (1929–2001)

Professor and director, designer, and performer with PlayMakers Repertory Company. Teacher of design and technology. Degrees from UNC-Chapel Hill (BA, MA) and additional graduate study at Northwestern University. Joined the faculty in 1956 as technical director and scene designer. This multi-talented faculty member, in whose honor the Tom Rezzuto Guest Lectureship Fund was established, retired as Professor Emeritus in 1987.

Susanna Rinehart (b. 1964)

Lecturer and popular performer with PRC, appearing in the dual roles of Frau Overbaer and Mouserinks for five seasons in *The Nutcracker,* among many other productions. Teacher of acting and theatre history and literature. Degrees from UNC-Chapel Hill (BA, MFA). Appointed in 1989 and left in 1999 to join the faculty at Virginia Polytechnic Institute and State University.

Scott Ripley (b. 1962)

Assistant Professor and performer with PRC. Teacher of acting. Degrees from the United States Naval Academy (BS) and the University of California, San Diego (MFA). On the faculty from 2008 to 2012, he left to join the faculty at University of Connecticut after which he joined the faculty at the University of San Diego.

Michael Rolleri (b. 1959)

Professor and Production Manager for PlayMakers Repertory Company. Teacher of technical direction and production, in particular machining, rigging, and health and safety. Degrees from Dennison University (BFA) and UNC-Greensboro (MFA). He was appointed to the faculty in 1986 and has been the mastermind behind the smooth running of numerous productions since that time.

David Rotenberg (b. 1950)

Visiting Associate Professor and Artistic Director 1981–1983 (co-artistic Director with Greg Boyd in 1982–1983). Teacher of acting and directing. Degrees from The University of Toronto (BA) and the Yale University School of Drama (MFA). Left in 1983 to return to New York City and soon thereafter joined the faculty at York University in his native city of Toronto, Canada.

Brian Russman (b. 1967)

Lecturer and crafts artisan for PRC. Teacher of costume crafts including dyeing, painting, and millinery. Degrees from the University of Nebraska-Lincoln (BFA) and The Ohio State University (MFA). He was on the faculty from 1994 until 1997 when he moved to New York where he spent 12 years as design assistant and associate designer on Broadway shows. He won the 2001 Primetime Emmy Award for Outstanding Costumes Emmy Award for *Life with Judy Garland*. In 2009 he joined the faculty of the Carnegie Mellon University School of Drama as an Associate Teaching Professor.

Daniel E. (Dan) Scuro (1933–1996)

Assistant Professor, Director of the Department of Dramatic Art's Laboratory Theatre, and Director of Undergraduate Studies. Teacher of directing and theatre history and literature. Degrees from St. Mary's College in Notre Dame, Indiana (AB), Xavier University, Cincinnati (Med) and The Ohio State University (PhD). He was appointed to the faculty in 1979 to strengthen undergraduate production and served until 1981 after which he relocated to New York City.

Gwendolyn Schwinke (b. 1959)

David G. Frey Fellow and Assistant Professor, and Resident Vocal Coach for PlayMakers Repertory Company. Teacher of voice, speech, text, and dialects with an emphasis on the Linklater, Feldenkrais, and Colaianni methods. Degrees from Drury College (BA) and Illinois State University (MFA). A long-time company member of Shakespeare & Company (Lenox, MA), she joined the faculty in 2019.

Michael Sexton (b. 1963)

Visiting Assistant Professor and director (*The Man Who Came to Dinner*) for PRC. Teacher of acting. Degree from Columbia University (BA). On the faculty in the 1998–1999 academic year, when he also directed *The Balcony*, performed by graduate and undergraduate students, in Historic Playmakers Theatre. Artistic Director of The Shakespeare Society from 2005 to 2017, he became Director of The Public Shakespeare Initiative when it moved to The Public Theatre.

Ann Shepherd Sheps (1914–2002)

Lecturer and Director of Graduate Actor Training, and resident actor with PRC from 1975–1982 after a distinguished career as an actress, mainly in New York City.

She began performing using her given name, Shaindel Kalish, and in the mid-1930s adopted Ann Shepherd as her stage name. Her long list of Broadway credits ended in 1973 when she moved to Chapel Hill with her new husband, Dr. Cecil Sheps, Director of the Center for Health Services Research at UNC-Chapel Hill. She was on the faculty from 1975 to 1982.

Penny Pence Smith (b. 1943)

Adjunct Instructor and Project Coordinator for PRC's annual benefit while pursuing doctoral studies at UNC-Chapel Hill in the School of Journalism and Mass Communication (now the Hussman School of Journalism and Media). Teacher of arts management. Degrees from the University of Washington, Seattle (BA), the University of Southern California (MA), and UNC-Chapel Hill (PhD). She was on the faculty from 1996 to 1998.

Aubrey Snowden (b. 1982)

Teaching Assistant Professor in the Department of Dramatic Art. Teacher of perspectives in theatre, script analysis, and directing. Degrees from Manhattanville College (BA) and Brown University/Trinity Repertory Company (MFA). She directs regularly for the Wilbury Group in Rhode Island, the Kenan Theatre Company (KTC), and the Professional Actor Training Program, at UNC-Chapel Hill. Joined the faculty in 2019.

Kenneth P. Strong (1958–2010)

Adjunct Assistant Professor and popular PlayMakers Repertory Company member, fondly remembered for his performance as the Aviator in *The Little Prince*. Teacher of acting. Degrees from UNC-Chapel Hill (BA, MFA). His acting career included productions in many regional theatres. From 1991 to 1995, he was a member of PRC's acting company after which he moved to New York City. His appointment to the faculty began in 2002 after several additional years acting on stage and in film. He was highly regarded as a performer and teacher until his untimely death in 2010.

Mark R. Sumner (1923–2017)

Professor and Director of the Institute of Outdoor Drama from 1964 to 1990. Teacher of playwriting. Degrees from UNC-Chapel Hill (BA, MA). Playwright and mentor to other writers, particularly writers of outdoor dramas and pageants, he retired in 1990.

Bill Svanoe (b. 1938)

Adjunct Professor. Teacher of writing for the stage and screen after a career acting and writing for the stage and screen. Degree from Oberlin College (BA) and graduate study at the University of Minnesota. On the faculty from 2002 to 2008, after which he returned to semi-retired life in California with his wife, the actress and director Joan Darling.

Linwood Taylor (Clifton Linwood Taylor, Jr.) (1941–2009)

Lecturer, Technical Director and Head of Graduate Program in Technical Production, and Scene Designer for PlayMakers Repertory Company. Teacher of theatre design and technology. Degrees from Campbell University (BA) and UNC-Chapel Hill (MA, MFA). Served on the faculty from 1978 to 1987, after which he worked as an art director and production designer for film and television.

Patti Worden Thorp (b. 1960)

Lecturer and Communications Director / Development Officer for PRC. Teacher of theatre management. Degrees from UNC-Greensboro (BFA) and the Yale University School of Drama (MFA). On the faculty from 1992 through 1997, when she left to lead the capital campaign for Raleigh Little Theatre. She returned to PRC as chair of the Friends of the PlayMakers Advisory Council when her husband, Holden Thorp, became the tenth chancellor of UNC-Chapel Hill in 2008.

Robert W. Tolan (b. 1935)

Visiting Professor and Producing Director for PRC from 1983 to 1985. Teacher of theatre management. Degrees from the University of Missouri-Kansas City (BA), Bowling Green State University (MA,) and Purdue University (PhD). He left in 1985 to be producing director for Heritage Artists, Ltd. at the Cohoes Music Hall in New York state.

Craig Turner (b. 1947)

Professor and movement coach / fight director for PlayMakers Repertory Company. Appointed in 1985, he retired as professor emeritus in 2017. Teacher of movement, stage combat, and Tai Chi. Degrees from Wichita State University (BA) and The Ohio State University (MFA). Notably, he has worked on more productions for PlayMakers Repertory Company to date than any other individual—including 139 credits for movement. He also directed *LuAnn Hampton Laverty Oberlander* for PRC in the 1986–1987 season, and appeared as an actor in both *Much Ado About Nothing* and *Prelude to a Kiss*.

Adam Versényi (b. 1957)

Professor and Department Chair (2014–present) and Senior Dramaturg for PlayMakers Repertory Company (for more than eighty productions). Teacher of theatre history and literature, he is the founder and editor of the online journal, *The Mercurian: A Theatrical Translation Review*. Degrees from Yale University (BA, MFA, DFA). He was appointed to the faculty in 1988.

Zannie Giraud Voss (b. 1964)

Assistant Professor and Managing Director 1994–1996. Teacher of Theatre Management. Degrees from Louisiana Tech University (BA), Texas A&M (MBA) and

Aix-Marseille III Graduate School of Management - IAE, France (PhD). She left in 1996 to join the faculty at Duke University and to serve as producing director of Theater Previews. She is currently Chair and Professor of Arts Management and Arts Entrepreneurship at Southern Methodist University where she is also Director of the National Center for Arts Research.

Jeffery West (b. 1948)

Adjunct Assistant Professor and acting company member with PRC, beginning with the role of Austin in *True West*. Teacher of acting. Degrees from The College of William and Mary (BA) and the University of Virginia (MFA). On the faculty from 1990 to 1992, he left to teach at Duke University and to continue his busy acting career in the Triangle area.

Neil Williamson (b. 1975)

Adjunct Associate Professor and Technical Director (after a year as Assistant Technical Director) for PRC and DDA. Teacher of technical direction. Degrees from East Carolina University (BA) and UNC-Chapel Hill (MFA). Also a lighting and scene designer who designed for PRC's Summer Youth Conservatory (SYC), including *Oliver!*, and Triangle area theatres. On the faculty from 2006 to 2009, when he left to join the professional staff at Elon University.

Jiayun Zhuang (b. 1976)

Assistant Professor and dramaturg for PlayMakers Repertory Company. Teacher of theatre literature and performance studies. Degrees from the Beijing Academy of Drama (BFA, MFA) and the University of California, Los Angeles (PhD). A member of the faculty from 2010 until 2017 when Dr. Zhuang returned to her home in Beijing, China, where she continues to write plays in both Chinese and English.

Appendix III

MFA Degree Recipients, 1975 to Present

The first MFA degrees were awarded in the Department of Dramatic Art in May 1975. The specializations have changed as have the number of students admitted each year. Since 1995 the specializations have been Acting, Costume Production, and Technical Production. In 2012, the Professional Actor Training Program (PATP), which generally enrolls 6 to 8 actors in each class, started accepting a new class in two consecutive years after which a year is skipped.

1975

Boykin, Nancy Jo	Acting
Coleman, Joseph Frank	Directing
Downing, David Fortune	Scene Design
Dunthorn, Deborah Ashley	Acting
Gangotena, Araminta Casper "Ari" (aka Ari Casper-Silverman)	Costume Design
Greer, Dallas Kenneth	Acting
Greer, Margaret Tucker (aka Maggie Tucker)	Acting
Hurst, Gregory Squire	Acting
Jankavs, Gunta Gabrielle	Acting
Kerley, Michael Vincent	Directing
Kohr, William Wallace	Playwriting
Olivier, Sally MacLaughlin "Sam"	Scene Design
Phialas, Mark Campbell	Acting
Ranson, Rebecca Hargett	Playwriting
Rawluk, Nicholas Joseph	Scene Design and Technology
Sidden, Duane Kermit	Directing
Stancik, Valerie Deibler	Acting and Directing
Ussery, Richard Lee	Acting
Phelan, Kathleen G.	Directing

1976

Ball, Randolph Newton	Scene Design
Collins, Rebecca Hiatt	Acting
Davis, Donna Byrd	Acting
Fritz, Lana	Costume Design
Jackson, Susan Jane	Acting
Keeler, Leroy Heany (aka Brian Keeler)	Acting
Lipton, Lawrence Jay	Directing

Nielsen, Mark S.	Playwriting
Persinger, Philip Burwell	Playwriting
Phialas, Deborah Strang	Acting
Sutherland, James Malcolm	Acting
Wiles, Julian Dukes	Scene Design

1977

Arnold, Henry Ormond "Chip"	Acting
Bergen, Reed Lindemuth	Directing
Bergmann, Adam E.	Playwriting
Blake, Bonnie Sue	Acting
Dacons-Brock, Karen Denese	Acting
Dixon, Michael Bigelow	Playwriting
Ford, Anne Denise	Directing
Foster, Lipton Arlene	Acting
Geiss-Karas, Sandra	Acting
Glenn, David M.	Scene Design
Goodman, Robert Earl	Directing
Lockner, David John "Sparky"	Lighting Design
Shepherd, David Allan	Acting
Shepherd, Barbara Buchanan	Acting
Silver, Ross Lawrence	Directing
Von Werssowetz, Lawrence	Scene Design
Westbrook, Teresa Roberts	Acting

1978

Adamson, David A.	Directing
Arthur, George Nathan	Technical Direction
Chappell, John Wayne	Acting
Corlett, Donald Frederick (Fred)	Directing
Corriher, Kurt Dennis	Acting
Daggan, John Ralph	Acting
Ferguson, Jule Britt (aka Jule Selbo)	Acting
Finchley, Joan	Acting
Goin, Kennith William	Acting
McKay, Jeffrey Lynn	Technical Direction
McNally, Brian James	Acting
Metz, Catherine Taylor (aka Catherine Taylor)	Acting
Rankin, Dorothy Hutaff	Acting
Smith, Mary Faye Listerman (aka Faye Listerman)	Costume Design
Westbrook, Daniel Joseph	Acting
Woodfield, Nancy Jane (aka Nancy Davis)	Costume Design

1979

Beeson, Donna Lee	Stage Management
Boardman, Cynthia Ann	Technical Direction
Burleson, James Gillam	Acting
Colwell, Knox Cadman	Directing
Couch, John William "Jack"	Acting
Fitz-Simons, Haskell Lee	Acting
Liske, Anne Louise	Acting
Taylor, Clifton Linwood	Scene Design
Wiesenfeld, Marcia Ann	Acting

1980

Bailey, Randall James	Technical Direction
Barrett, Jane Ellen	Acting
Eason, Vicki Ernesta	Acting
Faris, Lamis Beasley	Acting
Gallagher, John Joseph	Acting
Gillott, Thomas George	Acting
Loggins, James B.	Acting
Mitchel, Cynthia Leigh	Acting
Mitchell, Belinda Mathews	Technical Direction
Nelson, Karen Lee	Acting
Randall, Edna Rae	Acting
Ryder, John	Acting
Shannon, Michael Taylor	Acting
Vick, Carol Josephine	Costume Design
Yeuell, Michel Sawyer	Costume Design

1981

Coble, Anne McKay	Scene Design
Cureton, Gordon Tobias	Acting
Douglass, Margaret Brewington	Acting
Gillett, Hamilton Lathrop	Acting
Gullucci, John Thomas	Acting
Jenkins, Nancy Hollis	Costume Design
Maurer, Martha Beauchamp "Marci"	Acting
Miles, Paul Dean	Acting
Newsome, John Wilber	Acting and Directing
Nowell, Susan Marilyn Polk (aka Susan Polk)	Acting
Pait, Larry Richard	Acting and Directing
Philyaw, Michael Greg	Acting
Royster, Laura Janelle	Acting

Shannon, Martha Wilson (aka Martha Wilson)	Acting
Teal, Danny Herman	Acting
Trimble, Emile Jean	Acting
White, Kathleen, Mary (Kathy W. Cole)	Technical Direction
Wilkins, Suzanne Young	Costume Design
Thurston, Robert Joseph	Lighting Design

1982

Derbyshire, Charles Edward	Acting
Hansen, Elizabeth, Ann	Acting
Johns, David Thomas "Tom"	Technical Direction
Johnson, Cynthia Ann	Acting
Larson, Cathy Ann	Acting
Moessen, Maria Louise	Acting
Romero, David Glen	Acting
Strong, Kee Fortes	Acting
Strong, Kenneth P.	Acting
Wieb-Ellis, Monica Renate	Acting

1983

Baggott, Shaun Lee	Acting
Behre, Michael Ray	Acting
Blalock, LarryAllen	Technical Direction
Chin, Ping-Ping "Pamela"	Costume Design
Clayson, Laurel Elizabeth	Costume Design
Freeman, L. Anthony	Acting
Jones, Herman Laverne	Acting
Riccillo, Charles Lawrence	Technical Direction
Schultz, Suzanne M. (aka Suzanne Reed)	Costume Design
Stefan, Deborah Susan	Technical Direction
Williamson, Hubert Lee	Acting

1984

Mitchell, Robert Dale (aka Dale Mitchell)	Acting
Newhall, Deborah Clark	Costume Design
Tyson, John Warren	Acting

1985

Andrews, William F.	Technical Direction
Catotti, Charles Giacomo	Technical Direction
Cumpsty, John Michael (aka Michael Cumpsty)	Acting
Meisle, Kathryn Hunt	Acting
Niemiec, Mona Rita	Acting

O, Kyong-Sook	Technical Direction
Orzolek, Robert Louis	Technical Direction
Seitz, Anne Jeanette	Acting
Wilson, Wendy Beth (aka Wendy Barrie Wilson)	Acting

1986

Cook, Mitz Christine	Costume Design
Feltch, John Franklin	Acting
Gottlieb, David Norman	Acting
Goulet, William Lawrence	Acting
Hertsgaard, Peter Conrad	Acting
Knowling, Lorraine Denise "Lori"	Technical Direction
Melocchi, Wanda	Acting
Williams, Shelley Irene	Acting

1987

Carter, Christopher West	Technical Direction
Franklin, John Owen	Costume Design
Harris, Kate	Acting
Hotaling, Brian Alton	Acting
Murphy, Robert Kennard	Acting
Reihl, Arthur Alan	Technical Direction
Royce, Rebecca	Acting

1988

Conover, Constance Van	Acting
Fitzsimmons, Thomas Matthew	Acting
Haj, Joseph C.	Acting
Hecht, Deborah Anne	Acting
Proctor, Melissa Tracy	Acting
Whalen, David Allen	Acting

1989

Addison, Bernard Kelvin	Acting
Gagnier, Derek Paul	Acting
Garvey, Thomas Peter	Acting
Milan, Candice Marie	Acting
Pappageorge, Demetrios Gregory	Acting
Rinehart, Susanna Cecilia	Acting
Selby, David Alan	Technical Direction
Young, A. Eben	Acting

1990

Benedict, LisaDiane	Acting
Passarella, Lynn Elizabeth	Acting
Pounders, Steven Craig	Acting
Reider, Joel Carmi	Acting
Ryan, Matthew David	Acting
Schneider, Jennifer Karen	Costume Design

1991

Carlos, Aaron	Acting
Gunning, Thomas Patrick	Acting
Herrera, Pilar Padin	Acting
Knight. Aaron James	Acting
Krell, Daniel John	Acting
Potter, Samuel Clinton	Acting
Robison, Blake Elliott	Acting

1992

Altmeyer, Timothy Charles	Acting
Eaton, Eve E.	Acting
Haggerty, Stephen Aloysios	Acting
Newman, Emily	Acting
Pratt, Craig Thomas	Technical Direction

1993

Anderson, Carol Elizabeth	Acting
McIver, Charles Anderson	Acting
Morrissey, Connan Lynn	Acting
Peters, Donna Lynn	Acting
Sellon, Andrew W.	Acting

1994

Du Fretay, Brett Halna	Acting
Eis, Mark Ransom	Acting
Ellingson, Barbara Anne	Acting
Hartwell, Michael S.	Technical Direction
Music, Ronda Karen	Acting
Stephano, Alexander Yannis	Acting
Watt, Kristine	Acting

1995

Betz, Jefrey Allen	Acting
Cartmel, James Patrick (Pat)	Acting

Hunziker, Lisa York	Costume Production
Johnston, Laurie Paige (aka Paige Johnston)	Acting
Jones, Cheryl Lisa (aka Fiona Jones)	Acting
King, Michael Houston	Acting
Langdon, Brent Alan	Acting
Suhr, Christine C	Acting
Wagenseller, Edwin Holt	Acting

1996

Brooks, David Michael	Acting
Carr, Thomas Dacey	Acting
Christopher, Brian "Bostin"	Acting
Clay, Kim Ann	Acting
Fike, Raymond Leon	Technical Production
Huang, Hui-Lin "Lydia"	Costume Production
Hunter, Michael Gerard	Acting
McCauley, Katherine Liles	Technical Production
Munro, Andrew Bruce	Technical Production
Padilla, Julie Antoinette (aka Julie Padilla M)	Acting
Rosenfeld, John Eric	Acting
Strimling, Jody Lynn	Acting

1997

Babbitt, Michael W.	Acting
Dillard Jr., Peter Fielding	Acting
Dumond, Rodney Harrison	Technical Production
Fleming, Matthew Thomas	Acting
Kramer, Robert F.	Acting
Malogrides, Heather Lynne (aka Heather Grayson)	Acting
Malos, Erika Eve (aka Erika Keil)	Costume Production
Pettigrew, Craig Leroy	Technical Production
Roberts, Shannon R.	Acting

1998

Butler, Kevin Maurice	Acting
Cornell, Jeffrey Blair	Acting
Davis, Lisa Anne	Costume Production
Fishell, Julie	Acting
Hendrick, Michelle CT	Acting
Jung, David S.	Acting
Klein, Timothy Patrick	Acting
Knight, James Donald	Technical Production
Romans, Bruce Marshall	Acting

Shively, Sarah Elizabeth	Acting
Tower, Joshua A.	Acting
Underwood, David George	Technical Production

1999

Bodine, Gregory Oliver	Acting
Duke, Jason Bonnard	Technical Production
Frederic, Michael Wayne	Acting
Lapaglia, Michael Salvatore	Technical Production
Martinson, Kerri L.	Costume Production
McIver, Lucy Grey Cole Wilson	Acting
McLeod, James R.	Technical Production
Murray, Benjamin Denis	Acting
Schancupp, Jonathan David	Acting
Schulke, Jeri Lynn	Acting
Vail, Jason Daniel	Acting
Yao, Kun-Chun "Gwendolyn"	Acting

2000

Nance, Patricia Fay (aka Tricia Lapaglia)	Technical Production
Rosas, Anthony E.	Technical Production
Wagner Denise E.	Costume Production

2001

Hylton, Elizabeth "Beth" Grey	Acting
Marchelya, Rita Lynne	Acting
Moon, Hannah	Acting
Riva, Denis Pasquale	Acting
Savage, Peter G.	Acting
Shoup, David Eric	Acting
Tricarico, Lia J. (aka Lia Carpenter)	Costume Production

2002

Albrecht, James P.	Costume Production
Camper, Brooks Ann	Costume Production
Ellis, Lauren G.	Acting
Linton, Marcy J.	Costume Production
Maxfield, Adam Michael	Technical Production
Miller, Matthew Bradford	Technical Production
Moeller, Harold Todd	Acting
Nestor, Siobhan Ann	Costume Production
Parkinson, Deanna Anita (aka Deanna Henson)	Acting
Prichard, Jason T.	Technical Production

Robinson, Brian C.	Acting
Stern, Marc Alexander	Acting

2003

Glaser, Valerie A.	Technical Production
Wigginton, Laura Paige (aka Laura Bullock)	Costume Production

2004

Ausberger, Sara Ann (aka Sara Stockton)	Costume Production
Days, Pia Davida	Acting
Heitman, Caroline Marie "Carrie"	Acting
Houghton, Brooke Ariel Moyer	Acting
McKay, Mollie E. (aka Monja McKay)	Acting
Meanza, Jeffrey T.	Acting
Meredith, Brian William	Acting
Monroe, Kara M.	Costume Production
Shaffner, Edward David "Ted"	Acting
Van Der Linde, Cornelia Maria "Lien"	Technical Production
Walsh, Karen Beth (aka Karen Beth Walsh Rullman)	Acting
Wiley, Michael Lafon	Acting

2005

Blann, Joshua A.	Acting
Campbell, Todd	Technical Production
Chen, Judy W. "Wei Fen"	Acting
Giardina, Vincent R.	Acting
Hamm, Zachary D.	Technical Production
Hyatt, Rebecca	Costume Production
Kalagher, James E.	Acting
Lawrence, Todd W.	Technical Production
Leonard, William B.	Technical Production
Lemming, Iisha L. (aka Iisha Paschall)	Costume Production
Sheaffer, Adam M.	Acting
Smith, Brandon M.	Acting
Stanley, Tiffany R. (aka Tiffany Rebecca Royale)	Acting

2006

Garman, Herbert G.	Technical Production
Jacob, Jennifer A.	Costume Production
Papa, Jade Ryan (aka Jade Bettin)	Costume Production

2007

Alirez, Reina T. (aka Reina Alirez Herberger) — Costume Production
Bedford, Heather M. — Technical Production
Cardwell, Eric D. — Technical Production
Kendall, Anne F. — Technical Production
Korey, Erin B. (aka Erin Korey Proud) — Costume Production
Patterson, Matthew M. — Acting
Priest, Nikolas F. — Acting
Reeves, Allison Sarah — Acting
Steak, Charles Anthony — Acting
Tarver, Loyd E. (aka Estes Tarver) — Acting
Williams, Danika D. — Acting
Yost, Marla E. — Acting

2008

Bagley, Michael A. — Technical Production
Brookshire, Jane Elizabeth "Janie" — Acting
Friedlander, David Gardner — Acting
Henderson, Mark Spencer — Costume Production
Larson, Kalen J. — Technical Production
Mason, Emily N. (aka Emily Heilig) — Costume Production
Schultz, Wesley J. — Acting
Spann, Marshall Bryant — Acting
Stephens, Heaven Chijerae — Acting
Stutts, William G. — Acting
Taylor, Christopher J. — Acting
Hunter-Williams, Kathryn — Acting
Williamson, Neil A. — Technical Production

2009

Blakeney, Jacki (aka Jacki Armit) — Costume Production
Longwell, Kyle Raymond — Technical Production
Merola, Laura Paulette — Technical Production
Phillips, Amanda Louise — Costume Production
Weger, Brian Daniel — Costume Production

2010

Aberts, Todd Christopher — Technical Production
Bowie, Prince Tatt — Acting
Handley, Randy Lynn — Costume Production
Hebron, Sarah Elizabeth — Technical Production
Jones, Joy Ametra — Acting

Murphy, Matthew Anthony	Acting
Page, Amy Allison	Costume Production
Perez, Flor De Liz	Acting
Powers, Jason Allen	Acting

2011

Brummer, John	Acting
Gonzalez-Garcia, Kahlil (aka KG Garcia)	Acting
James, Rodney Wayne	Technical Production
Kieffer, James G. "Jimmy"	Acting
Ledbetter, Derrick Michael	Acting
Miller, Marianne Catherine (aka Marianne Phelps)	Acting
Parks, Shanna Ileah	Costume Production
Whitley, Alice Catherine	Acting

2012

Blinn, Kenneth C.	Technical Production
Fleming, Claire	Costume Production
Rousseau, Jordan McLane	Technical Production
Smith, Kaitlin Fara (aka Kaitlin Fara)	Costume Production
Spensieri, TJ Michael	Technical Production

2013

Batteast, Danielle Dina (aka Dee Dee Batteast)	Acting
Bolton, Brett Thomas	Acting
Didion, Kelsey Ahlene	Acting
Dreher, John Michael	Acting
Ellis, Thomas Wiggins	Technical Production
Garner, Matthew	Acting
Paxton, Katherine Scarlett	Acting
Tobin, Joshua David	Acting

2014

Chelnov-Snitow, Tania Marya	Acting
Claridad, Nathaniel Perdigon	Acting
Connerley, Dawn Alex	Technical Production
Corral, Adrienne Marie	Costume Production
Epting, Michael Bryson	Technical Production
Garegnani, Brandon John	Acting
Johnson, Nilan Stuart	Acting
McClernan, Candyce Ann "Candy"	Costume Production
McHugh, Patrick O'Leary	Acting
Pates, Laura	Technical Production

Pelz, Leah Elizabeth	Costume Production
Renko-Clarkson, Kelly	Costume Production
Rodgers, Chad Nicholas	Technical Production
Ryan, Nicholas Shannon	Technical Production
Searle, Maren Stavig	Acting

2015

Chukhina, Denise Ann (aka Denise Dietrich)	Costume Production
Dobson, Colleen Faulling	Costume Production
Finn, Beckett Michael	Technical Production
Hodges, Corinne Anneliese (aka Corinne Doss)	Costume Production
Zervas, James W.	Technical Production

2016

Abbenante, Erin Renee	Costume Production
Amick, Benjamin Kyle (aka Kyle Amick)	Technical Production
Cox, Carey Leigh	Acting
DeCandia, Gregory George	Acting
Donoso, Jorge William	Acting
Hughes, William Thurston	Acting
Keener, Katherine Wallace	Costume Production
Oleksy, Kevin Joseph	Technical Production
Strange, Caroline Brittany	Acting
Yoder, Arielle Elisa	Acting

2017

Altman, Allison C.	Acting
Bailin, Daniel Marc	Acting
Castaldi, Kathleen Sara "Katy"	Acting
Curns, Benjamin Richard	Acting
Curry, Adam John	Technical Production
Epps, Maxalenson Michel "Max" (aka Max Hilsabeck)	Costume Production
Kovaka, Mackenzie S.	Technical Production
Mastain, Schuyler Scott	Acting
Plonski, Emily Maria	Costume Production
Walton, Jacob	Technical Production
Washington, Myles (aka Myles Bullock; Myles B)	Acting

2018

Ankerich, Robin Leighanne (aka Robin Burton)	Costume Production
Bentley, Michelle	Costume Production
Billik, Scott Joseph	Technical Production
Torkelson, Erin	Costume Production

2019

Culbertson, Geoffrey Robert	Acting
Dhamija, Rishan	Acting
Givens, Alex Michael	Acting
Hansen, Thomas "TJ"	Technical Production
Latimer, Jennifer "Jenny"	Acting
Leonard, Shanelle (aka Shanelle Nicole Leonard)	Acting
Mirzayan, Christine	Acting
Parks, Tristan Andre	Acting

2020

Bosco, Emily	Acting
Davis, April Mae Arlene	Acting
Haynes, Brandon Herman St. Clair	Acting
Huebert, Cami	Costume Production
Keyes, Sarah Elizabeth	Acting
Love III, Richard Allen "Rocky"	Technical Production
Pohl, Nathaniel S.	Technical Production
Poole, Adam	Acting
Reckford, Samantha	Costume Production
Reichard, Jane	Costume Production
Soldat, Danielle	Costume Production
Spensieri, Kyle Matthew	Technical Production
Toot, Daniel Hill	Acting

Appendix IV

PlayMakers Repertory Company Administrative Leadership, 1975 to Present

Artistic directors oversee all of the aesthetic aspects of regional theatres, working closely with directors, production managers, and the creative teams. They have a partnership with the specialists who handle the business side of the operation. Generally known as managing directors, the person in that role oversees all of the administrative functions, including marketing, fundraising, finances, and general operations.

1975–1978

Joseph Coleman, who earned an AB and an MFA from UNC-Chapel Hill, was appointed as PRC's first Managing Director in 1975. Arthur Housman, chair of the Department of Dramatic Art, identified his skill as a director and his youthful energy as assets, which they proved to be during the early years of the professional company. He left Chapel Hill in 1978 to pursue opportunities as a director but subsequently resumed administrative positions, first as Chairman of Financial Service Centers of America (FiSCA) and since 1989 as President of RiteCheck Check Cashing.

1978–1982

Edgar B. Marston became Managing Director after serving as Executive Director of the North Carolina Arts Council from 1968 to1973, and director of the North Carolina Division of the Arts in the Department of Cultural Resources from 1973 to 1978. During his tenure, using his background as an experienced arts administrator, he standardized administrative procedures, increased the size of the business-related staff, and supervised a much-needed renovation of Playmakers Theatre—often giving credit to the MBA he had earned at UNC-Chapel Hill. When he left PRC, he became the Administrative Manager of UNC's Extension and Continuing Education Division.

1982–1983

George A. Parides (1942–1996) joined PRC as Managing Director after serving as administrative director of the McCarter Theatre in Princeton, New Jersey. He left after one season to join the professional staff of the North Carolina Theatre Conference (NCTC) where he had a long and successful tenure as director of NCTC's Theatre Arts Division of the North Carolina Arts Council. NCTC presents an annual recognition, the George A. Parides Professional Theatre Award, in his honor. The UNC-Chapel Hill Department of Dramatic Art received the award in 2007 and PRC in 2020.

1983–1985

Robert W. Tolan, with titles including both Managing Director and Producing Director, led the administration of PRC from 1983 to 1985. He brought with him experience from senior positions at the Cincinnati Playhouse, the Virginia Stage Company, the Fulton Opera House, and Studio Arena Theatre. When he left in 1985, he became the producing director of the Cohoes Music Hall in Cohoes, New York.

1985–1986

Jonathan L. Giles was managing director of PlayMakers Repertory Company during the 1985–1986 theatre season. After earning a graduate degree in arts administration from UNC-Greensboro, he began his association with PRC as a box office assistant in the 1983–1984 season and was promoted to the position of audience development coordinator the following season, 1984–1985. He left Chapel Hill in 1986 to manage a professional choir based in Washington, DC, after which he worked with the noted avant-garde composer and artist Meredith Monk.

1986–1989

Margaret Hahn held a series of administrative positions with PRC, beginning as literary manager (1983–1984), then as Associate Producing Director (1986–1987), and finally as Managing Director (1987–1989). Milly S. Barranger, while on the faculty at Tulane University, had met Margaret Hahn when she was studying for her MFA degree at Tulane and recruited the talented administrator to join PRC. She left Chapel Hill in 1989 to take a position as a theater specialist at the National Endowment for the Arts in Washington, DC.

1989–1991

Regina F. Lickteig served as Administrative Director for PRC from 1989 to 1991, after spending the 1988–1989 season as production stage manager. Her considerable administrative skills were an advantage during a time when the company faced both a period of growth and budgetary constraints. She left PRC in 1991 to become Managing Director of the Marin Theatre Company in Mill Valley, California.

1991–1994

Mary Robin Wells was appointed Interim Managing Director in fall 1991 and served until the spring of 1993, when she was named Administrative Director. She remained in that position through the 1993–1994 season. After completing her MBA in the Kenan-Flagler School of Business at Chapel Hill, she relocated to Louisville, Kentucky to pursue opportunities in consumer marketing, eventually holding senior positions with companies including Sonic, Dennys, and Hertz.

1994–1996

Zannie Giraud Voss was PRC's Managing Director from 1994 to 1996. She had spent the previous two years at the Alley Theatre in Houston, Texas as Associate

Manager (after earning her MBA degree from Texas A&M). Prior to that, she had worked for the Mark Taper Forum and the Ahmanson Theatre in Los Angeles in audience development. When she left in 1996 she became a member of the faculty and producing director of Theater Previews at Duke University. She currently serves as a professor in the Meadows School of the Arts at Southern Methodist University.

1996–1998

Donna Bost Heins (aka Donna Bost Prichard) has served PRC in a variety of roles. She was General Manager from 1991 to 1993 after which she returned to Juilliard School Department of Vocal Arts and the Associate Administrator for three years. She returned to PRC as Administrative Director in 1996. Before coming to UNC-Chapel Hill, she was Stage Manager for the Juilliard School Drama Division during the academic year and General Manager of the Weston Playhouse in Weston, Vermont during the summer season. When she left in 1998, she worked as an administrative and small business consultant.

1998–2000

Mary Lee Porterfield came to UNC in 1998 to become Managing Director of PRC. She brought experience as a performing arts administrator at the Alley Theatre in Houston, Texas, where she served as Associate General Manager. When she left Chapel Hill in 2000 she changed careers, becoming an administrator with the North Carolina Division of Child Development and Early Education.

2000–2006

Donna Bost Heins (aka Donna Bost Prichard) returned to PRC as Managing Director from 2000 to 2003. When she was assigned additional administrative responsibilities, she also received a new title—Executive Director—a position which she held until 2006. When she left PRC she initially hoped to develop a family-oriented theatre in the Research Triangle area, but ended up using her considerable administrative skills as a small business consultant, before becoming a principal with Theatre Consultants Collaborative.

2006–2007

Rob Franklin Fox was General Manager of PlayMakers Repertory Company from 1999 until the end of 2006–2007 season. When Donna Bost Heins departed he became the senior member of the administrative staff—the culmination of ten years in a variety of positions with PRC, beginning in 1997 when he was assistant box office manager. He left in 2007 to become the director of the University's Institute of Outdoor Drama.

2007–2008

Heidi Reklis began working for PRC as an office assistant while she was in her first year as a Chapel Hill undergraduate, pursuing a BA with a major in linguistics.

After receiving her degree in 2004 Heidi Reklis became Assistant General Manager. She was promoted to General Manager in April 2007 and remained in that position for nearly eight years. For the 2007–2008 season, Reklis was the senior administrative manager for nearly a year, after which she continued in her role as General Manager until July 2014. Since then she has worked for Bain and Company where she manages a team that supports support Bain's partners and senior managers in their east coast offices.

2008–2014

Hannah Grannemann (aka Hannah Grannemann-Isaac) was PRC's Managing Director from 2008 to 2014. She modernized the box office and other business practices drawing upon the expertise she gained as Associate Managing Director of the Yale Repertory Theatre in New Haven, Connecticut (like PRC it is closely aligned with an academic unit) and through earning two graduate degrees from Yale University, an MFA and an MBA. She left PRC in 2014 to become the Executive Director of the Children's Theatre of Charlotte.

2014–2016

Michele Weathers was named Interim Managing Director in 2014 after spending fifteen years as Associate Producer for the North Carolina Theatre in Raleigh, North Carolina and three years as the Managing Director at Theatre Raleigh. She left in 2016 to become the Managing Director of the Barrington Stage Company in Pittsfield, Massachusetts. Weathers subsequently returned to Raleigh in summer 2017 as executive director for Carolina Ballet.

2016–2020

Justin Haslett was Managing Director for PRC in 2016 to 2020 after working in theatre administration for the Huntington Theatre Company and at the Merrimack Repertory Theatre. He left in fall 2020 to consult in strategic operations and management, including the arts, in North Carolina and throughout the East Coast.

2020–2021

Joseph "Joe" Emeis joined PRC as General Manager in October 2018, relocating from Washington, DC where he had been Director of Ticket Sales and Audience Services at the Studio Theatre. Drawing on his experience working in the arts and restaurant services, he is responsible for overseeing all administrative activities until a new managing director is named.

Index

A Christmas Carol, 2017–2018.
Ray Dooley as the Storyteller.
Costume Design by Bobbi
Owen, Set Design by Jan
Chambers, Lighting Design by
Dominic Abbenante. Photo-
graph by HuthPhoto. Courtesy
of PRC.